TO BE HONEST

Voices on Donald Trump's
Muslim Ban

TO BE HONEST

Voices on Donald Trump's Muslim Ban

SARAH BETH KAUFMAN, WILLIAM G. CHRIST, AND HABIBA NOOR

TRINITY UNIVERSITY PRESS
SAN ANTONIO, TEXAS

Trinity University Press
San Antonio, Texas 78212

Book design and composition by Amnet Systems
Cover design by Anne Richmond Boston

ISBN 978-1-59534-951-4 paperback
ISBN 978-1-59534-952-1 ebook

Trinity University Press strives to produce its books using methods and materials in an environmentally sensitive manner. We favor working with manufacturers that practice sustainable management of all natural resources, produce paper using recycled stock, and manage forests with the best possible practices for people, biodiversity, and sustainability. The press is a member of the Green Press Initiative, a nonprofit program dedicated to supporting publishers in their efforts to reduce their impacts on endangered forests, climate change, and forest-dependent communities.

The paper used in this publication meets the minimum requirements of the American National Standard for Information Sciences—Permanence of Paper for Printed Library Materials, ANSI 39.48-1992.

CIP data on file at the Library of Congress

25 24 23 22 | 4 3 2 1

We dedicate this book to the many people who collaborated with us: the 172 interview respondents, four outstanding research assistants, university colleagues, funders, workshop participants, actors, directors, stage crews, museum staff, journalists, editors, grant and publication reviewers, and audiences. You are a part of this work and we celebrate you.

CONTENTS

CONTRIBUTORS

William G. Christ is one of the three co-researchers, writers, and producers who created *To Be Honest*. He is Professor Emeritus at Trinity University and has been writing about media education for over forty-five years. Dr. Christ was Chair of Trinity University's Department of Communication for 12 years and General Manager of the jazz radio station KRTU-FM for 14 years. Christ's interests lie in bridging the gap between the liberal arts and professional education, and he has written or edited seven books and published or presented over 125 book chapters, articles, essays, and papers on media representation, education, literacy, and assessment. He has held leadership positions in three national and international associations and served on the editorial boards of two prestigious journals. In 2006, he received Trinity University's Distinguished University and Community Service Award. In 2012, he was awarded the Broadcast Education Association Distinguished Education Service Award, which is given to an individual "who has made a significant and lasting contribution to the American system of electronic media education."

Stacey Connelly is the originating dramaturg and director of *To Be Honest*. She took her PhD in theater at Indiana University, then studied in Berlin as a fellow of the German Academic Exchange Service. As Associate Professor of Theater at Trinity University, she teaches performance, theater history, and text analysis. She also directs for Trinity's theater program and has worked as a director and dramaturg for AtticRep Theater, San Antonio Public Theater, The Classic Theater Company, and the McNay Art Museum. Her articles on German theater and political drama have appeared in regional and national journals. In 2019, with Trinity's Center for International Engagement, she was one of three professors to launch Trinity in Germany, a seven-week program on German culture, literature, and theater.

Sarah Beth Kaufman is one of the three co-researchers, writers, and producers who created *To Be Honest*. She is an Associate Professor of Sociology at Trinity University, where she writes and teaches about culture, knowledge, criminality, race, and the law. She was an investigator and mitigation specialist in New Orleans during the 1990s, helping to secure reduced sentences for impoverished capital murder defendants, before completing a PhD in sociology at New York University. Her first book, *American Roulette: The Social Logic of Death Penalty Sentencing Trials*, is the first systematic ethnography of death penalty trials in the United States. She has also published in such journals as *Law and Social Inquiry*, *Qualitative Sociology*, and *Critical Criminology*. In 2020, Dr. Kaufman was awarded Trinity University's Distinguished Teaching and Research Award for an Early Career Faculty Member. In 2021, she and Habiba Noor initiated Trinity University's Story Lab, an interdisciplinary project that merges storytelling with social research.

Tahir Naqvi acted in the first performances of *To Be Honest,* in the role of Hari, a Sikh man who is mistaken to be Muslim. He received a PhD in Anthropology from the University of California, Berkeley, and is an Associate Professor of Anthropology at Trinity University. Dr. Naqvi's research and teaching focus on post-colonial and urban studies, addressing questions of state power, belonging, urban space, and the production of political identities in South Asia and the Muslim world. His forthcoming book is based on years of fieldwork in Karachi, examining the Muttaheda Quami Movement (United Nationalist Movement), and the transformation of political allegiances in Pakistan after partition.

Habiba Noor is one of the three co-researchers, writers, and producers who created *To Be Honest.* She is a Visiting Assistant Professor in the Department of Education at Trinity University where she teaches courses on Social Justice and Urban Education, among other classes. Noor received a PhD in Media and Cultural Studies from the Institute of Education in London, where her arts-based research focused on Muslim youth and their relationship to news of the "War on Terror." From this research, she argues that contemporary Muslim identity politics are intrinsically linked with the politics of representation, and that the burden of representation poses a paradox for Muslim communities as it can be at once alienating and create opportunities for agency and community development. Noor wrote the curriculum for the "Muslims in Brooklyn" oral history project at the Brooklyn Historical Society. In 2021, she and Sarah Beth Kaufman initiated Trinity University's Story Lab, an interdisciplinary project that merges storytelling with social research.

Van Wagner was one of four Trinity University student researchers who collaborated on the interviews that became the basis for *To Be Honest*. After graduating from Trinity, she obtained a Master of Arts in Religion with a concentration in the History of Christianity from Yale Divinity School. Wagner's research interests include conservative evangelicalism in the United States, specifically as it intersects with civil religion and conservative political engagement.

INTRODUCTION

Sarah Beth Kaufman, William G. Christ, and Habiba Noor

> *"There are moments in history when a particular event brings the various ideologies and beliefs prevailing in a culture into sharp focus . . . By paying careful attention at moments like this to people's words, one is able to hear the way these prevailing ideas affect not only individual lives, but also the culture at large."*
>
> —Moisés Kaufman, "Introduction" to *The Laramie Project*[1]

This multidisciplinary, multi-format book was created from the ideas of scholars, artists, religious and political leaders, and everyday Americans. Following the work of Moisés Kaufman and the Tectonic Theater Project, we make visible the wake left by a cultural event: Donald Trump's 2015 campaign promise to enact a "Muslim Ban." Readers will find that the book begins, after this Introduction, with a script titled *To Be Honest: Voices on Donald Trump's Muslim Ban* (hereafter *To Be Honest*), that we created from interviews with people in San Antonio, Texas, during the lead-up to the 2016 presidential election. The words of *To Be Honest* are drawn verbatim from the interviews, but the setting is an imagined space where the interviewees can hear each other. Written in 2017, *To Be Honest* has been performed in university classrooms, full-scale theater productions, and iterations in between. For those interested in exploring its meaning further, the script is followed by essays investigating themes in theater studies, media, culture, religion, sociology, criminology, and anthropology.

At this Introduction's writing, Donald Trump has been impeached for a second time. He was defeated by Joseph Biden in his attempt for a second term as president, but he also garnered more votes than any other Republican presidential candidate in history. Time will tell whether the 2020 presidential election will be remembered as a repudiation of Trumpism, or its vindication and solidification in the Republican party. Either way, Trump's influence will reverberate in America's political landscape for years to come. His presidency was staggering in the frequency and ferocity with which civil and democratic norms were broken, which left little time for processing. We hope this book will contribute to the retrospective work of sitting with and sifting through the impacts of such events.

Crafted from interview transcripts, *To Be Honest* does not solve the challenges that Trump's comments catalyzed. Rather, the play serves as a mirror that shows the diverse and competing views of a highly polarized moment. The work is divided into 17 episodes focusing on themes that emerged during the interview process, with a core narrative framed around the story of a 35-year-old we call Chris, a disabled U.S. veteran who had a transformative experience during his deployments in Iraq and Afghanistan. Chris describes becoming honest with himself, eventually experiencing emotions about war that set him apart from his officers. While witnessing Chris's transformation, audiences also observe conversations among grandmothers making sense of young people's political disconnection, university students talking about their families' prejudices, and Iraqi refugee seekers who clarify the heterogeneity of the Muslim experience. All of this takes place against the backdrop of a turbulent election period. Many of the play's short episodes are framed by news reports, from terrorist attacks in Baghdad to strident policy differences between the presidential candidates. It reminds us of the action-packed summer and fall leading to the 2016 election, filled with violence, emotion, and finally, an unexpected result.

In the remainder of this chapter, we introduce the play in its historical and disciplinary context and share our own surprising journey as academics-turned-playwrights. Amidst the many disturbing surprises of the Trump era, we found solace in the collaborative, creative work of listening and sharing the experiences of peers and strangers. We hope the play and subsequent chapters provide teachers, students, interfaith organizers, and others with fertile material for exploring a historical moment that captured our attention and our imaginations.

HISTORICAL CONTEXT

Our project grew in tandem with Donald Trump's rise to power, starting when we three researchers began an investigation into the anti-Muslim and anti-immigrant rhetoric of his 2016 presidential campaign. In late 2015, presidential candidate Trump's openly misogynist, nativist, and xenophobic comments dominated news of the election. As part of his bid to secure the Republican nomination for president, he promised to "shut down" Muslims from coming to the United States. His rhetoric, amplified by countless media outlets amidst fear of "extremist" violence, both real and perceived, challenged our assumptions on religious freedom in America, and became a central issue in the presidential election. Though Trump's presidency would later be characterized by state violence against migrants at the southern U.S. border and attacks on peaceful protesters, his scapegoat during the first phase of his ascension was Islam.[2] Indeed, among the first acts of the newly-elected President Biden in 2021, was a reversal of the "Muslim/travel ban," removing one of Trump's most objectionable executive orders.

Nearing the end of 2015, presidential hopeful Donald Trump had a slight lead in a competitive Republican primary race. Then, on December 2, 2015, Pakistani American Muslim Rizwan Farook and his wife Tashfeen Malik, who had immigrated to the United States from Saudi Arabia one year prior, perpetrated a mass shooting in San Bernardino, California. Fourteen people were tragically murdered. At a press conference in South Carolina five days later, Trump famously proposed a "total and complete shutdown of Muslims entering the United States." He said, "They have no respect for human life. So, we have to do something." For his supporters, this exclusion was a matter of national security. As Trump explained, "It has nothing to do with religion, it's about safety."[3] When Trump proposed banning immigrants from Muslim countries, some were shocked by a potential U.S. president discriminating against people on the basis of religion, in a country where religious liberty is a foundational principle. Others argued that the ban was a necessary method to prevent terrorist attacks. The topic of Islam in American political discourse is not new, interwoven in the history of imperialism in Asia, racial subjugation, Arab-Israeli geopolitics, and the "War on Terror." But for the most part, the notion of *excluding* Muslims from American civic life had been relegated to "fringe" groups in the twenty-first century.[4] Nonetheless, Muslims belonging in America became a topic of national debate in the lead-up to the 2016 presidential election. By early 2016, polls showed that Trump's proposal divided the country by political party, race, and religion; while almost 90% of Democrats disapproved of the proposed "ban," 81% of Republicans approved, as did over 70% of white evangelical Christians. Black and Hispanic Americans, Catholics, Jews, and Muslims also overwhelming disapproved.[5] The proposed ban was met with criticism from prominent members of the Republican party, including Mitch McConnell, Paul Ryan, and even Mike Pence. But once Trump's candidacy was established, party members' objections dwindled.

Trump's position marked a significant shift in how to name and identify the source of violence at the root of terrorism. After the 9/11 attacks, President George W. Bush was careful to make a distinction between the violent acts and the religion of Islam, so as not to demonize the religion. In a speech, he reminded audiences that "millions of our fellow citizens are Muslim. We respect the faith. We honor its traditions. Our enemy . . . hijacked a great religion."[6] In contrast, Donald Trump identified the root of the violence as Islam itself. In March of 2016, he said, "I think Islam hates us."[7] Believing Muslims to be dangerous requires the homogenization of 1.8 billion people spread out across all regions of the globe, with different relationships to tradition and modernity and representing a range of cultural traditions and ethical positions. Characterizing this diversity has been a challenge, in part because the racial and ethnic categories on the U.S. Census do not accurately represent how many Muslims see themselves. In particular, the Census categorizes Arabs, Iranians, and North Africans as white, which many see as a form of erasure.[8] Pew survey data estimates that 3.45 million Muslims live in the United States, thirty percent of whom identify as white, 23% Black, 21% Asian, and 6% Hispanic. Eighty-two percent are American citizens, with roughly a quarter from families who have been in the United States for three generations or longer. Approximately two thirds support the Democratic party, with 30% calling themselves politically liberal.[9]

A week after he became president, Trump signed an executive order to exclude many Muslims from the United States. The order banned entry to foreign nationals from seven predominantly Muslim countries—Iran, Iraq, Libya, Somalia, Chad, Syria, and Yemen (later changed to Iran, Iraq, Libya, Somalia, Sudan, Syria, and Yemen)—for 90 days, suspended entry to the country of all Syrian refugees indefinitely, and prohibited entrance of any other refugees to the United States for 120 days.[10] After successful court challenges to the ban, the Supreme Court ruled by a 5-4 vote in June 2018 that a revised version of the ban could stand. The revised version banned foreign nationals from the above countries from entering, and added North Koreans, as well as Venezuelan officials and their families.[11] Some argued the addition of these countries did not disguise the fact that the ban targeted Muslims.[12]

This project began before the ban was institutionalized. In the tradition of historical sociology,[13] we were trying to understand history in the making, capturing the way that meaning is created as important events unfold, recording "culture on the street" as Raymond Williams[14] would have it, before positions become ossified in policy.[15] We recognized the "Muslim ban" as a potentially pivotal moment in discourses of race, migration, and belonging, and were eager to understand the range of beliefs and experiences that it produced. Our goal was to create the opportunity for a cross section of people in a community to more deeply express their opinions beyond surveys noting whether they were "for" or "against" the ban.[16] When we accomplished this, we were struck by the passion and honesty of their words, and we wanted to share them publicly, beyond the usual scholarly audience. To do this, we turned to our colleagues in theater.

MAKING *TO BE HONEST*

The Interview Process

To Be Honest is a nonfiction drama that is composed entirely of excerpts from interviews with 172 Americans during the 2016 presidential campaign. The script immerses audiences in the conflicts surrounding Islam in

America by sharing real stories of neighbors from across the political and religious spectrum, including Evangelical ministers, members of the Sikh and Jewish communities, Catholics, Muslims, atheists, and others. In this sense, *To Be Honest* takes readers and audience members to foreign places in their own country, showcasing a remarkable array of lived experiences in a single American city. We were able to capture these experiences with help from a Mellon Foundation grant, which allowed us to conduct interviews for an intense 10 weeks in San Antonio, Texas, during the peak of the presidential campaign. With the assistance of four undergraduate students, we accessed diverse religious and political networks. We held focus groups and one-on-one interviews with members of religious groups in town. We set up interviews at senior and refugee centers, local universities, and with leadership from LGBTQ organizations and military personnel. Central to the success of our research was the diversity of our research team: young and old, with a variety of ethnic and religious backgrounds. We each drew on our own biographies to find commonalities with those we interviewed.

We designed a set of interview questions that we thought would elicit honest and open responses across diverse populations, appropriate for Muslims and non-Muslims, liberals and conservatives. This was no small task. We spent weeks thinking about exactly how to create questions that would allow dissimilar participants to speak candidly with our team. We explained to our student assistants that we would purposely build some ambiguities into the questions so that we could observe the variety of interpretations, but that we had to avoid non-purposeful ambiguities that would make the data impossible to analyze. Our student researchers were sometimes baffled by our methods, as they watched us argue over which of three synonyms to choose for a question about the past (all of which meant "the past"), or worried about how respondents would react to the word "fear." We trained them in open-ended qualitative interviewing, emphasizing how to minimize egos in order to give priority to participants' feelings and beliefs. Above all, we tried to impart that interviewees were the center of the interviews and that we were there to create environments where people could think out loud as they grappled with and tried to articulate their own attitudes and opinions. Eventually, we agreed on four main questions: 1) What have you heard about Islam during the presidential campaign? 2) Does this conversation remind you of others in history? 3) How did you form your ideas about Islam? 4) Have you ever experienced fear around these issues?[17]

San Antonio was an interesting city to conduct social science research on Islam in American politics because it is home to a growing Muslim population, large military bases, and evangelical pastor John Hagee, one of Donald Trump's most ardent supporters. It also has a sizable working-class population and is a "majority-minority city"—a city with a larger percentage of people who identify as Latinx than those who identify as non-Hispanic white—which is predicted to become increasingly more common in the United States.[18] In Bexar County, where San Antonio is located, Donald J. Trump/Mike Pence received 40.42% of the vote and Hillary Clinton/Tim Kaine received 53.74% in 2016.[19]

Contrary to the popular notion that Donald Trump cleaved the nation's conscience in two, our interviewees before his election show that Americans had already established deep and complicated relationships with ideas about citizenship, nationality, and belonging, entwined with notions about Islam. Bubbling just below the surface of civil discourse, our interviewees shared worries about their futures and that of the United States. These worries were not immediately forthcoming. As we talked with interviewees about Trump's statements, we noticed that many of them shifted course during the conversations. "I always felt like an American," said one Muslim interviewee, but "to be honest . . . I'm worried for the country's future." A liberal Democrat confessed that despite his professed opposition to Trump's position on Islam, "to be honest . . . I don't know what to think about Trump." "I've always been proud to be an American," one elderly Jewish woman told us, "but to be honest," she *was* afraid of Muslims. And on it went. Scholars describe expressions like "to be honest," "honestly," and "in fact" as "honesty phrases," often used when a speaker is asserting what they really think is an unpopular opinion. Such phrases mark the ways in which people negotiate their own ideas in relation to what they believe to be the norm.[20] Reading through the interviews, we noticed that "honesty phrases" were used quite frequently in about 1 out of every 5 interviewees. It was apparent that such phrases were used when an interviewee revealed something important about their views. The title of our play, *To Be Honest*, comes from this observation. Interviewees confessed that "to be honest," they had not been paying close enough attention to politics until their families were personally affected; that they occasionally had racist tendencies they had not examined until we asked; and some had to admit to being attracted to policy positions that their friends might find objectionable. This type of honesty lies in sharp contrast to the anonymity of the bulk of social media banter, and underscores the deeply personal nature of the interviews, when people trusted us enough to say where they *honestly* stood.

Though our research questions and direction of our potential academic papers were clear, our interviewees' responses moved us in unexpected ways. The people we spoke with confirmed the expected political polarizations, but were also funny, nuanced, and self-reflective. As the weeks of research continued, we marveled at the depth and passion with which our respondents answered our questions. We began to imagine a space in which these participants could hear each other. Regardless of their political or religious positions, all of our respondents' interest in the topic seemed personal, despite the fact that most of our interviewees were non-Muslim and had little or no contact with Muslims. We wanted to construct an imagined dialogue using the participants' words and create a space for audiences to bear witness to the ways in which this selection of voices responded to the messages of the campaigns. To bring this to the stage, we turned to our theater colleague, Stacey Connelly (see Chapter 1 in this volume).[21]

The Theater Process

Through previous collaborative teaching with Stacey, Sarah Beth and Habiba had learned that theater could be a powerful tool to showcase embodied, complex experiences. Stacey's teaching emphasized how a stage could engage the political, allowing audiences to confront human emotions without the filter of electronic media. Fear, suspicion, and fraught political climate surrounding Islam, immigration, and political violence necessitated complex civil discourse. But civil discourse in the public sphere was increasingly difficult to find. Though "new (social) media" in politics was at its inception and thought to be a potential boon for democratic participation in political discourse, it instead created polarizations and sites of contestation. After completing our interviews, we wanted to create an alternative forum for democratic engagement. With Stacey's help, we began to craft a script that was envisioned as a catalyst for conversation. We three researchers met in a room together over the course of four months, often several times a week and for several hours at a time. We consulted with our student researchers and eventually agreed on which small portions of our interview transcripts could best create the play's narrative, which formed around the central story of an interviewee who had experienced a dramatic personal transformation during his service in Iraq and Afghanistan. To say that we cut many compelling stories and experiences would be a vast understatement.

Our intense discussions resulted in a playscript that might be described as "documentary theater." As Stacey describes in Chapter 1, *To Be Honest* is similar to and distinguished from other types of this genre. Documentary theater typically requires some form of research to be used in crafting a script. That research, however, does not typically follow the methods of qualitative social science. And while qualitative social science depends on research, its findings are rarely presented as a play. We brought these two traditions together. We used exemplary sociological research frames, sampling, and qualitative interviewing to build what became a database of representative voices on an issue of particular significance to a community. Because our research follows our university's ethics code, we knew that we could not reveal the identities of the people we interviewed. Nonetheless, we were committed to allowing our interviewees to speak for themselves. We did this by assigning pseudonyms to each of our interviewees, editing the interviews for clarity and anonymity only, and otherwise leaving the words of our informants unchanged. Together with our dramaturg colleague, we turned our interviewee's stories into a narrative that is rooted in the performative arts. The power of the play is twofold. It attends to narrative structure, but it is also written using the direct words of real people in our city.

The script underwent several revisions during three workshops at Trinity University and one with members of the Church of Reconciliation in San Antonio. We invited many of our interviewees to attend and to give us feedback. When the play formally premiered at the San Antonio McNay Art Museum in September 2017, we were apprehensive as first-time playwrights, but we need not have worried. The museum staff had to turn people away for lack of seating. Over 400 people attended, with many willing to stand for the 70-minute performance as we held our breath. While the cast took their bows to a standing ovation, we watched audience members cry and embrace. Like all texts, the script did not produce the same impression for each audience member. Some reported that it was eye-opening; for others, it stimulated discussion on views that are seldom heard concurrently. A middle-aged white woman said to one of us, "I'm a councilperson in my ward and I had *no idea!*" Another said, "This has to be seen by *everyone.*" A Black woman who attended an early performance remarked that the play shows "the reality" of American views. A young Muslim man said that this was one of the first times he heard his own views voiced in a public setting.

The performance has since been staged in other formal theater settings around Texas—most recently at the Tobin Performing Arts Center in San Antonio—and used in university classrooms and interfaith settings. Throughout this process, we debated whether *To Be Honest* should be a staged performance that requires a cast of 22 along with publicity and production teams or performed more simply with group readings and non-actors. Luckily, we have experienced many variations in this regard. Through the outstanding staging and direction of three directors in particular—Stacey Connelly and Sam Gilliam of Trinity University and Vincent Hardy of St. Phillips University—we came to understand the tremendous affective power of live theater. We learned how actors and directors are not only performers, but also artists bringing their own interpretation to the script. We relished the way staged performance replaces the digital cacophony of Twitter threads and Facebook posts, whether in an educational setting with a small cast or in a full theater production.

We also found that the play is best experienced when there are structured opportunities for discussion at the end of the performance. To facilitate this, we developed a set of questions intended for small group discussions. After performances, audience members were invited to sit at tables and collectively discuss their reactions to the play. We then asked them to consider their own experiences and examine how they might be similar—or different—to the characters in the play and the people around them. These questions encourage audience members to participate carefully and deliberatively with those around them, and are included as Appendix B. We hope that you too might use them to reflect or ask others to join you in conversation.

Though the play has been performed many times now, we still have some qualms. *To Be Honest* is a challenging work. Some of the words and ideas of the characters may be disturbing. As the curators of real interviews, we sought to provide audiences with a snapshot of a political moment. Part of that moment was the intensification of anti-Muslim and anti-immigrant sentiments. A vital instance of this is emphasized in Episode 16 when one of the characters, Jay, shares a study from the Center for Security Policy, a think tank that is central to spreading anti-Muslim ideas.[22] Jay echoes their mischaracterization of sharia law as a totalitarian system and uses their research to suggest that Muslims seek to overthrow the United States.[23] These words are countered by the character Ellen, who is suspicious of such claims. We do not use Jay's words to legitimize or amplify anti-Muslim views, yet we know that certain audience members might nod in agreement when he speaks. In this sense, the script represents the range of views held by a diverse population, some of which we do not agree with. But our goal was to demonstrate how the 2016 election brought conflicting ideas into the mainstream, so we let these remain unchanged. By including such evocative statements, we challenge audiences to confront the contradictions circulating among us. *To Be Honest* allows audiences to listen to disparate voices unfiltered by the algorithms that keep people comfortable in "filter bubbles," a tricky proposition in any circumstance.

What to Make of the Book *To Be Honest*

This book makes *To Be Honest* available to educators, interfaith leaders, and anybody who might want to try to understand some of the many American experiences during a particularly fraught period in U.S. history. We encourage you to read, perform, discuss, *engage,* and try to be honest about your own unexamined stakes in this moment. To aid in this, we include essays written in our own disciplinary "voices," along with other collaborators on this project.

The book is divided in two parts. Part I contains the full script, and Part II is composed of six chapters providing readers with opportunities for additional engagement with some of the characters and ideas presented in the play. These chapters analyze the play's themes through a variety of lenses—written by scholars from the disciplines of Theater, Media and Communication, Religion, Sociology, and Anthropology—and include the play's co-authors, a director, and one of the actors. First, Stacey Connelly describes her experience as a theater scholar and director in helping shepherd *To Be Honest* to the stage. She calls attention to the craft of theater production, and the particular ways in which this play allows audiences to experience the political moment. In chapter 2, William Christ brings a political communication perspective to the ways that the news clips in the play function to set an agenda for the audience to think about what is important, to frame political issues, and to suggest which issues audiences ought to use to evaluate leaders. These three functions (agenda-setting, framing, and priming) are explored as the play reflects what seems an especially horrific news period during the summer of 2016.

Habiba Noor extends this analysis in chapter 3 by examining how the figure of the Muslim has been central to current political divides. As she details, the interviewees reflect core concerns about changes in American society: about the meaning of nationhood, shifts in uses of language, and expectations of women. In chapter 4, Van Wagner draws out interviewees' ideas about Christianity on the one hand and Islam on the other. Demonstrating evangelical Christian's commitment to strict and literalist Biblical interpretation, she argues that their commitment to binary and moral thinking shapes their judgements about civic and religious society more broadly, thus demonstrating the tenuousness of Americans' commitment to secularity in the twenty-first century.

In chapter 5, Sarah Beth Kaufman provides a critical criminological theory of the transformation of the category of "Muslim" in the public sphere. She argues that 2016 should be understood as a key juncture in the history of racism: when "Muslim" became an accepted criminal category in the United States. She discusses the ways in which the play's characters reflect this time period, when the United States "catches up" to European perceptions of Muslims as dangerous and disempowered citizens. Finally, the book finishes with an interview-style dialogue between Sarah Beth Kaufman and Tahir Naqvi. Naqvi is an anthropologist who identifies religiously as a Muslim, and also one of the actors who participated in *To Be Honest*. He was asked to embody a Sikh character, who is harassed as a result of being mistaken as Muslim. Kaufman and Naqvi's conversation illuminates the problematics and possibilities of theatrical representation.

Readers are welcome to read any or all of these chapters to explore *To Be Honest*. We hope you appreciate the variety of disciplinary perspectives as much as we have appreciated learning from one another. There are many additional themes in the play that we do not explore. We are curious to hear what else you find among the many, honest voices we present.

Part I

To Be Honest:
Voices on Donald Trump's
Muslim Ban

Habiba Noor, Sarah Beth Kaufman, and William G. Christ

Running Time:
Approximately 70 minutes, in 17 episodes

Episodes

Original Cast

Interviewer Sasha Faust/Jake Pursell

Myra Sam Gilliam/Judith Anthony

Patrick Nathan Stith

Chris Josh Segovia

Doug Alex Bradley/Chris Boneta

Barry Charley Price/ David Connelly

Lucy Taylor Mobley

Ana Yesenia Caballero

Jay Lawrence Coop

Karen Kathy Couser

Betty Susan Brogdon/Terri Pena Ross

Khadijah Elizabeth Cave/Yleana Wooten

Donny Rick Frederick

Joshua Torence White/Vincent Hardy

Hari Tanveer Arora/Tahir Naqvi

Saleem William Razavi

Ellen Linda Ford

Heather Julia Palmer

Marco Octavio de la Pena/Alejandro Cardona

Sarita Lopita Nath

Aliyah Caroline Arroyo/Yara Samman

Aden Bilal Zia/ Suhail Arastu

Pastor Bill Bill Schiller

CHARACTERS IN ORDER OF APPEARANCE

Note: This script was created entirely from verbatim interviews conducted in 2016. Names have been changed to preserve privacy, but otherwise interviews were transcribed as they were spoken and therefore are not corrected for standard English.

Interviewer Presents as an empathetic listener, neutral on all positions. The interviewer could be any gender and is preferably a college student or professor. In some performances, this role has been left out altogether.

Myra An educated, active Jewish woman in her early 80s. She is retired from a position of prominence in the Jewish community.

Patrick A heavy-set, white man in his early 60s. He works as part of a building maintenance crew and is reluctant to talk, claiming he's not political. When he does reveal his opinion, he uses humor.

Chris A Latino, disabled veteran in his mid-30s. He completed two tours of duty in Iraq and Afghanistan. He was injured in an explosion in combat and suffers from chronic pain due to back surgery, as well as PTSD. He speaks with great intensity when he's recounting these experiences.

Doug A 19-year-old white teenager who recently finished high school. He lives at home with his working-class parents. He describes himself as a conservative, Catholic Republican. He also considers himself a "gamer," spending lots of time playing video games with friends.

Barry A middle-aged, white college professor. He is very active in his church community and describes himself as a "principled" conservative.

Lucy A Black woman who is frustrated by the racist rhetoric of Donald Trump.

Ana A Latina, first-generation college student in her early 20s.

Jay A man in his mid-50s. He is a devout Christian and is retired from the military. He lives in the suburbs, and describes himself as a leader of conservative activists, part of a larger national movement.

Karen A well-off, Jewish professional woman in her 60s, married to an Asian man. She is well-traveled and sometimes feels alienated from members of her progressive Jewish community on the issue of Islam.

Betty A born-again Christian who participates in weekly Bible study. She comes from a working-class background.

Khadijah A Palestinian-American Muslim in her early 20s who wears hijab. She grew up in the U.S. as the eldest of seven children and describes herself as an activist and a lover of popular culture.

Donny A white, gay Republican man in his 60s. He is a retired civil servant and does not see being gay as his primary defining characteristic.

Hari A middle-aged, turban-wearing Sikh who has spent many years in the U.S. and is the husband of Sarita.

Joshua A Black man in his late 50s who works in education.

Saleem A Pakistani-American Muslim man in his 30s. He has a master's degree and works in finance. He grew up locally and lives with his family.

Ellen A Catholic woman in her early 60s who is dedicated to her work in social justice.

Heather A white college student who identifies with progressive politics. She laughs easily and is generally confident as part of a group.

Marco A Latino man in his late 20s. He identifies as an atheist and is still close with his Catholic family.

Sarita A South Asian woman in her 30s and the wife of Hari. She is a devout Sikh woman and wears a turban.

Aliyah An Iraqi woman and the wife of Aden. A college professor before leaving Iraq. She tends to be more trusting of the interviewer compared to her husband.

Aden The husband of Aliyah, a middle-aged Iraqi man.

Pastor Bill A middle-aged Evangelical pastor with national recognition. He seems to take some pleasure in courting controversy.

TO BE HONEST:
VOICES ON DONALD TRUMP'S MUSLIM BAN

Setting: A room where people are being interviewed. There is a large screen at the back of the stage where the slides and video are projected.

Media: Slides and/or audio are used to mark the beginning of each episode. Some are "title slides" only, where the title of the episode appears on a screen behind the actors. Other episodes begin with both title slides and other video and/ or audio, some original and some sourced. Sourced video and audio are provided in the notes and are denoted with quotation marks in the script. Original voice overs can be pre-recorded by a series of different people or read live on or off stage by the Interviewer or a narrator.

1. INTRODUCTION

Before lights fade up, the video of Trump's Muslim ban plays. As it plays, the actors from the first scene come on stage with the interviewer, who is positioned to see the actors and audience. The actors are looking at the interviewer.

Video starts.[24]

TRUMP (in video)

"Donald J. Trump is calling for . . . now listen you've got to listen to this because it is pretty heavy stuff . . . and it is common sense and we have to do it. Remember the poll numbers . . . 25%, 51%, remember the poll numbers . . . okay, so remember them . . . so listen . . . Donald J. Trump is calling for a total and complete shutdown of Muslims entering the United States until our country's representatives can figure out what the hell is going on. We have no choice. WE HAVE NO CHOICE."

Lights come up.
Slide of Donald Trump and Hillary Clinton fades in.[25]

INTERVIEWER

Thanks so much for meeting with me. I am studying how the religion of Islam is being talked about during this presidential campaign. We're interviewing people from all over the city. Of course, there is no right or wrong answer. The questions we are asking you are the same we will ask everyone. Everything you tell me will be kept anonymous. If we quote you in any of our reports or publications, we will change your name so that no one will be able to identify you as the speaker. Thanks for coming. We really appreciate your time. (*Pause*) So tell me: A lot has been said about Islam in this election. What have you heard?

Interviewer sits to listen.

MYRA

I'm not sure I really even think that religion is a proper topic of discussion in presidential politics. I really don't.

PATRICK

Life's changed in America. It's not like it was 20 or 30 years ago.

CHRIS

I heard Trump the other day, sounded like he wanted to wage war on them Muslims again, going out and finding them.

DOUG

Trump really wants to try to make America safe, I guess. To be honest, I think his immigration plans are actually pretty good.

BARRY

Personally? I don't believe terrorism is an existential threat to the United States nowadays unless Russia blows a head gasket and launches its nukes.

LUCY

The whole "Make America Great" means "Make America White."

ANA

Trump said so many comments, not just towards Muslims, but like, Mexicans.

JAY

People ask me, "Is Islam a religion of peace or a religion of violence?" I answer, "Yes" because it's both. Islam you never know.

KAREN

Their treatment of women was beyond belief.

BETTY

I don't really like to tell people my business, but when they ask, I want to be honest with them. They said, "Who are you voting for?" I basically said, "I'm voting for the lesser of two evils."

KHADIJAH

Someone asked me once who are you voting for. Honestly, I'm like I'm going to vote for the person that's rhetoric doesn't get me killed.

DONNY

I don't hear a lot of what's called *moderate* Muslims standing up for moderation.

HARI

Often times I've heard, "Hey terrorist, get out of our country."

JOSHUA

I am not really just one thing, I am what I am, I am anything, I am a Christian, I am a Muslim, I am all that.

SALEEM

(*Slightly frustrated*) There always seems to be like this need for like this big great enemy, and right now it's the so-called caliphate.

ELLEN

I think people in general are scared of what they don't know.

MYRA

I mean, we could be discussing terrorism, which is, you know, not only Muslims. I mean, who blew up the building in Oklahoma City? A good, red-blooded American.

PATRICK

(*Pause*) This is the worst I've ever seen. I don't know who to vote for. I'd rather write in Donald Duck. (*Chuckles*)

2. DEPLOYED

Title slide fades in.
Chris is on stage by himself.

CHRIS

My name is Chris. I'm 34 years old, retired Army. A couple deployments to Iraq and Afghanistan, combat deployments. When I first signed on to the military, my intention was to kill, kill, kill—right? With cold blue steel, I'm just ready to go and seek revenge, whatnot. I was wounded in August of 2006 in Afghanistan, and that's what kind of ended my military career. I broke my back and my face, separated my shoulders. They nursed me back to health and then I was no longer of use to them, the Army. My first appointment I could shoot anything and everything that I wanted to with whatever I wanted to. I know I might be a little scatterbrained right now, it's been a while since I've talked about this type of shit. It's been a long while.

3. MILLENNIALS

Title slide fades in.
Millennials (Heather, Doug, Ana, and Marco) are sitting together.
Myra, Karen, and Ellen are sitting together in a separate group.

MYRA

Shakes hands with Karen and Ellen.

Nice to meet you, I'm Myra.

KAREN

I'm Karen.

ELLEN

I'm Ellen.

Focus shifts.
The millennials do not shake hands while introducing themselves.

HEATHER

Hey, I'm Heather.

DOUG

I'm Doug.

ANA

My name is Ana.

MARCO

Marco.

HEATHER

I think that people from our generation have been fed like this idea of Islam that's very, like it oppresses women and it's anti-liberal and it's anti-intellectual and it's violent, and so like that's been the way that the media and everything has talked about Islam since we were kids, cause we're in this, you know, post-9/11 world of consciousness. That's like what the environment is that we've grown up in. They'll like maybe see it as maybe more prone to violence than Christianity. (*Pause*) At the time of 9/11, I was too young to understand, and I feel like the first time I actively considered Islam . . .

MARCO

All my friends that like I used to play like Xbox with, it's always, the whole like using explosives in that game just automatically make a joke about Islam or Allah Abu-Akbar, you know. Like suicide bombers.

HEATHER

I used to watch the show *24* . . . . It's about a counter terrorist organization and, I was watching it in like third or fourth grade with my dad. It was like my treat after flute lessons.

MARCO

I listened to like a lot of angsty punk rock music and there was one band that I really liked. I don't know if anyone knows NOFX. It's one of the early punk rock bands, but yeah. They have a lot of songs that are against Muslims, like there's one like, "No Fun in Fundamentalism," "72 hookers."

DOUG

Does everyone remember the comedian, Jeff Dunham, who had the puppets? And he had the one, "Achmed the Dead Terrorist."

Laughter from the group, remembering.

HEATHER

Yeah, in seventh grade . . . I went to a Christian private school for a year, and everyone was very angry. And everyone's just like, "Obama is Muslim!"

MARCO

I vividly remember 9/11. It was the first time . . . . It was the first time I saw my dad crying and that is traumatizing for any eight-year-old. I didn't understand what was going on, I didn't understand the significance of the building falling down. But I remember being quite disturbed because I could see how upset my parents were. And you know, how do you explain that to an eight-year-old?

ANA

I posted a meme of Donald Trump with Hitler's mustache, and someone commented, "That's *not* what he's preaching." I'm like, "What *is* he preaching? He's preaching hate toward a specific group, telling them that they have to wear specialized identification. Hitler did the same thing. That's a comparison." They're like, "No." I'm like, "Well, unfriended."

MARCO

I don't ever unfriend anybody on Facebook. But, an ex-girlfriend of mine from middle school posted something about Obama's Muslim agenda is the reason why that attack happened. I deleted her.

DOUG

It's actually my first time ever paying attention to a presidential election. I've heard some of our friends say, "I don't like Trump or Hillary. I'm not going to vote for either one of them." But it's still a good thing to get involved in politics, since we're at such a young age right now and it's our first . . . . We could actually vote now.

Others exchange skeptical looks as Doug speaks
positively about Trump.

(*A little defensively*) Whatever Trump wants to say, he's going to speak his mind. Trump doesn't really have a filter. He doesn't have that politician filter. That's one thing I really do like about Trump is if he disagrees with something, he's going to let the people know. I think it's better for any politician to be honest and speak their mind.

Shift focus to Ellen, Myra, and Karen.

ELLEN

My granddaughter is 21. She started dating a young man from Libya. I said, "Do you know about Libya?" She goes, "No, where is it?" They don't read newspapers. Everything is a sound bite. Everything is on an iPod or an iPad or Facebook.

MYRA

My grandson got very interested in Buddhism. He said to me, "I know now how I'm going to live: peace and I don't have to be concerned about everything." I sat there and I said, "Well, I don't believe that. You have to stand for something. You have to make the world a better place." He said, "You are so Jewish." I said, "Yes!"

4. LEARNING FOR YOURSELF

Title slide fades in.
Three men (Jay, Saleem, and Joshua) are standing separately from one another as they speak to the audience.
They do not respond to each other's words.

JAY

I'm retired Lieutenant Colonel Jay James, military. Prior to that I was a teacher. Served over in the Middle East for three rotations and got exposed to Islam up close and personal. Came back out of that in one piece thankfully. (*Pause*)

SALEEM

My name is Saleem. I moved to this city when I was about 15. I've been to Pakistan like five or six times, and my wife is from Pakistan.

JOSHUA

I'm Joshua. I am a native, went to high school here. I was in the military for a while, for six years, I was in the military. I was a Christian at the time.

JAY

I studied Islam, I didn't study it in school. I read a book by Daniel Pipes over in the Desert Storm in '91 and it resonated with me. It talked about the coming tide of Islam here in the United States. At the end of the day, that book told me intellectually that there was far more to this than I really knew.

SALEEM

When I moved here I kinda got closer to my religion because, really, I should say because of 9/11. Just because it pushed me closer to, I should say my people, to kind of seek refuge in that. Whereas going outside I would hear all these things, so the peaceful aura of a masjid was something that I craved back then.

JAY

I was led to begin to read the Quran and read the Hadith and study Islam. It became very apparent to me the bill of goods that America's been sold and what I'd been told in my days serving in the military. We knew very little about Islam, and the strategy we had to try to defeat Islam was not appropriate.

JOSHUA

At that time, I had never even read a book cover to cover. Just had never read one. I just happened to run up on the book *Autobiography of Malcolm X*, in a hotel or something. Someone had the book on the bed, I just looked at it. So, I started thumbing through it and read it. I was like, wow. (*Pause*) Went to college, got my bachelor's degree, master's, and doctoral degrees. I have written two books. I have been in education now for twenty years.

SALEEM

Starting like a few weeks after 9/11, there was a string of arson attacks on convenience stores, there were like nine in a row, like every other day there was one happening. All Muslim-owned businesses in this city. (*Pause*) So my dad has a convenience store and I used to work there, when I was in high school. Those people have seen me grow up. I was a kid, I was nobody. So I got asked about jihad and about sharia law and stuff. Out of this 17, 18-year-old kid they would ask these questions. My dad, he would just tell me to keep my mouth shut. But I don't know, I can't. In a way I guess it helped, because it forced me to do research, to learn things that I'd never cared for.

JOSHUA

I grew up a Baptist. Right here. We were the religion that our parents taught us to be, we didn't know any better. We went to church and all that kind of stuff, but when you start learning for yourself. . . . I think I'm probably the only one in my neighborhood that kind of went that way because being a Muslim is pretty much taboo. I know how beautiful it is, I know how beautiful all religions are. There is no bad religion. I had to come full circle. Now I can sit in the mosque, I can sit in the church, I can sit in the tabernacle, doesn't matter to me.

News slide of U.S. Senator Ted Cruz fades in
and voice over begins.[26]

SLIDE / VOICE OVER

Narrator: Texas Senator and 2016 Republican presidential candidate Ted Cruz calls a subcommittee hearing and states,

(Cruz audio): "The purpose of this subcommittee hearing is to assess the degree to which the administration is willfully turning a blind eye to radical Islamic terrorism, and the consequences for the safety and security of the American people."

5. POLITICAL CORRECTNESS

Title slide fades in.
Patrick, Doug, and Donny are sitting together.
Barry is standing apart.
Myra, Karen, and Ellen are sitting together.

DONNY

I'm Donny. To me, the left wants to pretend the bad parts of Islam do not exist and the right, the extreme right, only sees the negative part.

PATRICK

Name's Patrick. I'm 62 and I've seen quite a few elections. I vote Democrat pretty much every time. Union working man and stuff. Union's always been for the working man. Then again, the Democratic views are getting kind of faded now. There seems to be a more anti-Christian movement. It's okay to say negative things about Christianity in our society. It's not politically correct to say negative things about Islam in public.

DONNY

I'm Episcopalian which tends to lean left, and I tend to lean right. The Episcopal church, to me, has the opposite thinking than I do. They're trying to be politically correct. They're actually condemning their own while excusing the bad behavior. The church was on the wrong side of the Civil Rights movement. I think they're on the wrong side of *this* because they're not thinking this through. Not thinking it through.

PATRICK

You find yourself putting your guards more up. I think back in the days, like in the 60s and 70s, we didn't have to think about what we were going to say before we said it because you didn't want to hurt nobody's feelings or didn't want to say the wrong thing. People take it the wrong way. Back in the day I don't think they thought about it like that. It's just what it was. Nowadays, you say anything wrong, and they take it the wrong way.

BARRY

My name is Barry. I work in academia. We're so hypersensitive about race in this country. We should be able to say something like it was a six-foot Black guy who stole my purse without feeling like we're somehow being racialist or racist. It becomes almost irrational if you can't label something accurately.

DONNY

I don't think there should be a Hispanic Chamber of Commerce. I don't think there should be a Gay Chamber of Commerce, which there is. It should just be a Chamber of Commerce. They're pitting themselves against each other. I don't like that. I don't like that.

DOUG

I'm no fan of ISIS, but it gives me no right to hate an entire religion because of a few people.

PATRICK

(*Sarcastically, talking to Doug*) We don't have the right?! Yeah you still have the right to say it! It's your opinion.

DOUG

(*Responding to Patrick*) Okay, I have the right. I don't think I have the reasoning.

PATRICK

(*Muttering, shaking his head*) You dare speak your mind about maybe we shouldn't have Islam, then everyone's going to say you're a racist. You're a bigot.

BARRY

If there is a phenomenon of radical jihadists that tend to come for the most part from one section of the world, it doesn't strike me that that's necessarily Islamophobia as much as it might be prudence.

PATRICK

We elected our first Black president. Now we're going to try to elect our first woman president. It's kind of like we're just doing trends or fads. We need somebody in there that does something we need. That's what people like about Trump because he's not afraid to stick his foot in his mouth. He's just like the rest of us. It's kind of like yeah, we screw up.

BARRY

I see political correctness as a tactic on both sides of the ideological spectrum. My experience is that it is a tactic of the left used to shut down debate by shaming people or just defining them as bad, racist, sexist, whatever. Now again, if you go into political conservative circles, whether it's a church or just a bunch of rednecks on a hunting trip, there'll be a different kind of political correctness there. God forbid you raise the idea of climate change, for example, you're a nutjob if you say that.

Ellen is talking, with Karen and Myra listening.

ELLEN

I grew up as Catholic. I am not as active in the Church anymore, but the Catholic values are in me just like the grain is in the wood. I read a lot. I watch a lot. I'm learning about the prejudices of my close friends that were under the table until Donald Trump got the nomination. Just at the dinner table there are conversations that disturb me to no end with close, close friends. The way they echo some of Trump's comments about Muslims . . . . They have deep-seated prejudices that I wasn't aware of.

BARRY

As someone who is a principled conservative, I really think Trump has the potential to do great damage to certain principles I hold dear. And that, what do I do, I go home and tell my kids in years to come who I voted for? Can I in good conscience say that if I really think that he is temperamentally unqualified?

News slide of Sikh man who was attacked fades in and voice over begins.[27]

Narrator: September 2016. A Sikh man is attacked in Richmond, California. He is beaten, his turban removed, and his hair cut by a group of young white men.

6. SIKHS

Title slide fades in.
Sarita and Hari are standing next to each other.

SARITA

Hello. My name is Sarita . . . . This is my husband.

HARI

I am Hari.

SARITA

I've just never seen this country break apart so much, where it has become *justified* in going after communities. Whether it's the lesbian, gay community or the Muslim community. As a minority, I've never felt that I haven't belonged. I was raised in the U.S., my family came here when I was five, and I've always felt like this was my country, but this last year, it doesn't feel like my country. I am so sorry. [*Tears*]

HARI

People associated me as Muslim, and I'm not. I get branded in a negative way, just because people don't know, they look at me right away. It's the underlying assumption that people have: You must be Muslim, and you must be bad.

SARITA

My husband and I, we used to travel a lot. I don't like traveling anymore, honestly, because we are "randomly" (*sarcastically*) searched so many times. We were coming back from Florida, and from one terminal to the other I was searched four times. By the fourth time I lost it, and I said, "What is it that you want? You want my purse?" And I just dumped everything out because I had completely lost it.

HARI

I specifically remember after 9/11, my dad would just say, "Hey you can't go out. You shouldn't go out." In Oak Creek, Wisconsin, where somebody went into a Sikh temple and started killing because he thought they were Muslims. That's really what happened. He shot nine or ten folks who died. Policemen died, and policemen were injured.

SARITA

My son's only six years, he will be six next month, and he wears a turban. My son loves superheroes, he's like any other five or six-year-old. My daughters, they sing Kidz Bop all day long. Just as normal as regular American kids are, but to the public, seeing my husband and I both wearing turbans, and seeing these three children with us, they don't seem as normal.

HARI

It's not good for us to say, "Hey, don't hate me because I'm not Muslim. I'm a Sikh" because that implies that he's a Muslim, hate him. Sometimes I wish I had a shirt or a banner that says, "Don't hate me, I'm a Sikh, but even if I'm a Muslim, still don't hate me."

SARITA

Americans don't know who Sikhs are and we've been here for 100 years.

News slide of village being bombed fades in and voice over begins.[28]

SLIDE / VOICE OVER

Narrator: According to the Council on Foreign Relations, the Obama administration dropped at least 26,171 bombs in 2016. This means that every day, the U.S. military blasted combatants or civilians overseas with 72 bombs; that's three bombs every hour, 24 hours a day.

7. A U.S. SOLDIER, RIGHT?

Title slide fades in.
Chris is on stage by himself.

CHRIS

There was a couple things that got me there. One, it was seeing people, humans, treated like shit. I knew this dude. I had talked to him before. I had bought bread from him, we had worked together. He snatches this guy up and he says, "Well this is the bad guy, this is the bad guy." No it's not the bad guy. We take him in, hog tie his ass, take him in. The dude's crying and he's calling me by my name. I was just like, "I'm sorry. I don't know what the fuck's going on either." The dude's crying, he's scared, and then I get on the radio and I tell my buddy. I said, "Hey man, this is fucked up, dude." I said, "You know damn well this motherfucker had nothing to do with this shit. This is a fucking witch hunt. Fuck these dudes." I didn't know the lieutenant was still listening. The lieutenant comes in, he says, "All right, you. You want to go against me. You're going to watch him." I was on guard, I watched him for about four days. We had no food, we had no water, and I'm a U.S. soldier, right? (*Pauses*) Yeah, you're bringing up a whole lot of emotions, Interviewer. It's all your fault.

News slide of Orlando shooting aftermath fades in and voice over begins[29]

SLIDE / VOICE OVER

Narrator: June 12, 2016. Omar Mateen kills 49 people and wounds 53 inside Pulse, a gay nightclub in Orlando, Florida. Mateen calls 911 during the attack to pledge allegiance to ISIS and mentions the Boston Marathon bombers.

8. ORLANDO

Title slide fades in.
Khadijah, Donny, Sarita, and Ellen are standing alone.
Aliyah and Aden are standing together.

KHADIJAH

Hi. I'm Khadijah. My first reaction to the Orlando shooting was, "Oh my God. I hope it wasn't a Muslim." When I heard it was a Muslim I was like, "Oh no. Here we go. They're going to start harassing us again." The days after . . . I was in the store and there was a man who came up to me. I was scared because I could recognize he was gay, and I was scared that he was going to do something to me because he saw that I was a Muslim. I started trying to walk as fast as I could to my car because I got scared that he was going to do something to me. He told me, "I don't have a problem with you." (*With emphasis*) He came just to tell me he doesn't have a problem with Muslims for what happened.

DONNY

When something seems bad to be happening, it's not Islam's fault, it's someone else's fault. It's society's fault. It's the Republican's fault. It's white people's fault. Even with the massacre in Orlando, it was because he was gay. Well, as a gay person myself . . . evidently they're not finding any real evidence of that now.

ALIYAH

The man in Orlando . . . This is a psychopath really. He's not normal, nobody come there to kill about 100 people unless he is a madman. He's a psychopath, I think.

ADEN

We think he's a psychopath, no more than this. He's like them I think . . . . It had nothing to do with Islam. What Islam has to do with such things?

DONNY

The church I attend, after the Orlando massacre, the priest wanted to have members of the church to reach out to the Muslim community and dine with them. I had the opposite opinion. They should reach out to us. They're the one who . . . someone in their community has done something. They should reach out to the other side, not us constantly reaching. We're always asked to reach out for the other hand, but I never see the other hand reciprocating. That's disturbing to me.

ELLEN

People always say, "Well, why don't some of the Muslims speak out more?" Well, actually some of them do speak out, but the press doesn't pick up that kind of thing. The press wants to focus on the negative.

SARITA

If the shooter was Muslim, if the shooter was Christian, if the shooter was any religion, there is a mom who is going to cry for her son. There is a woman who is going to be losing her husband. There is the kids they're going to lose their parents by this. I don't know how people's mentality gets changed, and they're able to do all this stuff.

ELLEN

The Muslim community, why should they be expected to defend themselves to Christians when we have hate crimes done in the name of Christianity in this country? Do we hear criticism of the Christian community when the Klan did that, the American Nazi Party defends their whole principles on religious grounds?!

News slide of Muslims holding anti-terrorist signs fades in and voice over begins.[30]

SLIDE / VOICE OVER

Narrator: December 2015. Almost 70,000 Muslim clerics come together to pass a fatwa against global terrorist organizations, including the Taliban, al Qaeda, and the militant group that calls itself the Islamic State. They also ask that the media no longer identify the terrorists as Muslim since the acts of the terrorists go against the teachings of Islam.

9. DEBATING ISLAM

Title slide fades in.
Joshua, Jay, and Saleem return to their locations from the episode "Learning for Yourself."
Khadija and Donny are new voices.
They speak to the audience and cannot hear each other.

JAY

They're here to take over the country, the radical Islamists. Their hope and dream is that the Islamic flag will be flying over the White House instead of the flag of the United States of America.

JOSHUA

I have been in the Nation of Islam for twenty years, so when I hear about a "Muslim"—so to speak—being accused of committing a crime and blaming the entire religion of Islam, I just laugh. To blame the entire religion is laughable to me.

JAY

I heard of a fellow in the media that conducted a survey among Muslims in America. He asked, "If you had your preference between the American way of legal system or the sharia law, which would you prefer?" Two to one it was sharia law. We don't have a problem with you wanting to be here, but if ultimately your goal is to change the American legal system and the way we rule ourselves, then we do have a problem.

SALEEM

I mean it doesn't help that these jihadi organizations actually do exist. And they're doing what they're set out to do so that, that puts them in the news. (*Sarcastically*) Apparently sharia law is coming to America, that's what I've heard.

JOSHUA

It is funny because most people have never studied Islam. They know nothing about the Nation of Islam. If you study the history of slavery for example, the Africans that were taken from Africa to over here, they were Muslims.

SALEEM

You know my family, like most Muslims, well they're just kind of day to day, they just want to do their jobs and go home and watch television or just relax. There are a few of us that are activists like me, who actually will sit there and read books and form an opinion.

KHADIJAH

Islam in my opinion is my life. It's hard to listen to that rhetoric to say radical Islam. It's not even radical Islam because nothing they do is legitimately tied to Islam at all. I don't like the word "moderate" Muslim because I'm like what am I? The chilled-out person who prays five times a day?

JAY

Many Muslims will bury their head in the sand and say, "I'll pick and choose what I want to apply. Some of those things that Muhammad did, I don't want to know. I'm going to live my life peacefully." That's great. Sign me up. Give me a couple of million Muslims like that, but a Muslim doesn't get to define what Islam is, Muhammad does. Because it says, "Muhammad is the perfect Muslim."

JOSHUA

They say Jesus was a Muslim. If you understand what Islam is, "Islam" just means peace. It is an Arabic word. A Muslim is one who submits his will or her will to do the will of God. That's all a Muslim is.

DONNY

I had a Muslim roommate in college. Very difficult to get along with, very difficult . . . . A few years ago, he called me out of the blue. He told me that he had eight kids and that he was at Mississippi State University doing some kind of engineering. Then when I started talking about myself and I told him that I was gay and me and my partner we've been together for twenty-five years now. Click. That was the end of it. All I heard was dial tone.

*News slide of Pastor John Hagee fades in
and voice over begins.*[31]

SLIDE / VOICE OVER

Narrator: May 2016. San Antonio megachurch televangelist Pastor John Hagee tells supporters:
(Hagee audio): "I'm going to vote for the candidate that's going to make the U.S. military great again . . . for the party that is going to solve the immigration problem, not the one that has created the immigration problem . . . . I'm going to support the party that brings jobs back from China . . . not for the party that has betrayed Israel for the past seven years. If you can read a newspaper you know who I am talking about."

10. HOPE AND PEACE

Title slide fades in.
Pastor Bill and Betty are on one side of the stage speaking to each other.
Myra, Ellen, and Karen are sitting together on the other side.

PASTOR BILL

Hello. I'm Bill, pastor of the church here.

BETTY

My name is Betty. I totally have issues with the religion of Islam because I just don't think it's the truth. But with Muslims, I think reach out to them, treat them fairly so on and so forth, but for a totally different reason: proselytizing. I want Muslims to know what I feel is the truth, and it has hope and peace because whatever you believe, if you don't have hope and you don't have peace, then you've got nothing. When you're alone at night in the dark, do you have hope and peace? Most of the Muslims . . . all of the Muslims actually that I've spoken with don't have hope and peace.

PASTOR BILL

It makes me sad to think that there are people out there who think they need to strap a suicide vest to their bodies, or to their son's body, or to their daughter's body, or whatever, to go please their God. I mean, that's a horrifying thing to think that somebody actually believes that. Christ came so we could all experience His love, not so that we would all want to kill ourselves or kill other people.

BETTY

There are men in ISIS who have become Christians. They're hiding right now. Some are still in those countries, but they are posting something on our com-chat. They were passing out Bibles. They've actually been in prison, so they understand the cost. That's exciting to see how that works! God does not want that any should perish, but all would come to a saving knowledge of Him. Those are foundational truths of the Christian faith that Christ came for the whole of mankind, whether it's a radical Islamist or someone on the streets of this city.

PASTOR BILL

I tried to do a bridging activity where a friend of mine who is Muslim who is the outreach coordinator at a mosque had us over for Iftar Dinner, which is breaking the fast for Ramadan. I invited people. I made phone calls. We sent out an email. I presented it in front of the pulpit. One lady told me, "I don't know if I want to do that because I'm scared." I go, "Well, what are you scared about?" I was genuinely concerned. "Well, I'm afraid they might kill me." I said, "Are you fricking kidding me?" Then I got a text message from a different person. "I don't think we're going to go tonight." Why not? "Because of the date." I'm going, "What's wrong with the date?" "Well, there is three sixes in the date, 06-16-16." I'm going, "Are you fricking kidding me?"

The focus turns to the group of three women.
Karen still hasn't shared any information, but we can see her anger building.

MYRA

(*To Ellen*) There are extremists in every walk of life. Islam has the same kind of good life and Abrahamic traditional ideals that we *all* hold dear as the core of our value system.

ELLEN

Right wing Christianity still thinks that Betty Furness is the Virgin Mary, that the woman's place is in the home, and dinner better be on the table when I get there. American right-wing religion is full of anti-woman, anti-science, anti-progress.

MYRA

I've become very anti-fundamentalist religion. If you look at fundamentalists in Israel, I find them to be unreasonable and hateful. You can look at all religions and see that at different times. That's where I am now.

11. MY EVERYTHING

Title slide fades in.
Chris is on stage by himself.

CHRIS

We're at like this holding pen. This dude's hungry, I'm fucking hungry. I'm pissed, wondering what the fuck's going on. There's nobody I could talk to, right? Nobody I could fucking get out there. I had no radio; I was literally in a fucking pen with this dude. Then just by the grace of God I got my message out to this guy, and we were going to let this guy go, right? This guy came back clean, so we're taking him back out. He's in the back of my truck, he's got a bag over his fucking head, he's handcuffed, (*pause*) and I'm just about to have my son. (*Pause*) He's in the backseat and I tell him, "I'm taking you home buddy, I'm taking you home." He's just like, "Thank God." (*Pause*) I missed my son's birth, and at that point I was still desensitized. I still didn't really know the significance of my child's birth or anything, because I was fucking Iraq, I was Afghanistan, I was fucking war. But at that point, man, it was the most beautiful fucking time I had ever. It gives me fucking chills when I think about it. God it was beautiful, dude. It was beautiful. I think that's why the love for my son is so strong. Anybody that knows me, yeah, I might be a dick, but there's one thing. My son is my everything. (*Pause*) I've got a buddy, he's got nine tours under his belt and he hates everybody and anybody. He didn't experience anything like that, nor did he allow himself to, you know what I mean? Sorry, I just got a little excited.

News slide of Bernie Sanders and Muhammad Ali fades in and voice over begins.[32]

SLIDE / VOICE OVER

Narrator: June 3, 2016. Muhammad Ali dies. In a speech, Democratic presidential candidate and Senator Bernie Sanders says:

(Sanders audio): "To all of Donald Trump's supporters who think it is appropriate to tell us that they love Muhammad Ali but they hate Muslims—understand, understand that Muhammad Ali was a very devout Muslim who took his religion very seriously."

12. ERASED

Title slide fades in.
Joshua, Lucy, Pastor Bill, Saleem, Donny, Heather, Jay,
and Marco are all standing on their own.

JOSHUA

Malcolm X used to say that they don't kill you because you are a Muslim, they don't kill you because you are Christian, protestant, or Jew. They kill you because you are Black. The Powers That Be could care less that I am calling myself a Muslim. All they look at is the dark skin. That is how I am judged, that is how we are all judged, as Black people. Especially Black men. When I started studying Islam, it really taught me who I was. You would think we were only slaves, that we were only the hired help in America. (*Pause*) We were kings and queens. We were stolen from our country. We had empire and we were brought over here and broken down to basically nothingness. I just think of everything that we have gone through in this country as Black people, yet we are still here: the Tuskegee experiment, lynchings, Jim Crow, and you do all this to try to wipe us out. And I learned that really, Islam was the foundation of where I got that.

LUCY

Not only did you not wipe us out, but we got to the point where we have one that's sitting in the office as President right now. That's why you hate us so much.

JOSHUA

You can't ever wipe us out!

PASTOR BILL

I grew up in southeast Texas and it was pure white where I lived. I didn't grow up with Blacks or anything else. My great grandfather was in the KKK. We had all that horrible influence. My dad would not allow me to be prejudiced about anything ever. (*Pause*) I don't care who comes in, but they got to do it right. If they don't assimilate, they don't do well.

SALEEM

I was never confronted with racism growing up, but now there's a general attitude, people are either suspicious or they're extra nice. They're like *really* nice so that they don't feel—maybe they're still suspicious in their heart, but they don't want me to feel it.

DONNY

I just think we need to get past, for instance, Black Lives Matter. To me, that's a very hateful group. It's very racist, it's very hateful. It was built on a fictitious principle to start with because what happened in Ferguson didn't happen in Ferguson. There's no evidence that said we've got the hands up and all this stuff. It's horrible when somebody gets killed, but I think the reaction was way overreaction. The whole Black Lives Matter movement is based on a lie.

JOSHUA

The Black Lives Matter movement is a civil rights movement. The Black Lives Matter movement is the women's suffrage movement. The Black Lives Matter movement goes to freedom back in slavery days. This movement is not new.

HEATHER

I think there's a lot of fear like that in families about losing your family values that are supposed to be passed down. Like when I've dated Black men and when I've like shown interest in dating Muslims. It's like a threat to like my whiteness . . . . So if it's a white guy, I'm reproducing white children. If it's a Black guy, I'm reproducing Black children, which is bad. And a Muslim, he's going to change me from being Christian, like you're going to become Muslim.

JAY

(*Interrupting Heather*) That would be a real coup for a Muslim. If you marry a non-Muslim woman and you bring her to Islam, you've now just converted an infidel into a believer.

HEATHER

(*Not responding to Jay*) They're like why can't you date like a good ol' white Texas boy? They're basically saying, like white is pure. White is like good. I mean, they're not really saying this, but they basically are. My body's more like a vehicle and whatever guy I choose to be with, I'm reproducing whatever they are. (*Pauses and smiles*) My brother used to tell me—and this is really bad—but he's like "I'll give you $20 to bring home a Black guy, Heather." (*Laughter*) "You don't have to be dating him." And I'm like, "Oh, well, I'm actually dating one." (*Laughs*) "So I'll take the $20." (*Laughter*)

LUCY

Are we back to the thirties, forties, fifties, and sixties where my mere skin tone, my mere presence is offensive to you? That you'd stereotype me as being whatever you think I am just cause I'm Black, or just cause I'm Muslim? That's just the nature of being a person of color in this country . . . . I'm not gonna go cry a river at home because it happened to me. But to see tens of thousands of people lining up down the street to hear this man say these kinds of things is disturbing.

Marco walks on stage as Lucy says, "To hear this man say these kinds of things is disturbing."

MARCO

I dated a Muslim girl in high school. I was a freshman, she was a junior, which was interesting. She told me a lot about it, too. I was not particularly interested in her for her religious belief. She was beautiful. She was cool. Older chick, you know what I mean.

Lights fade out on rest of the others or they walk off the stage.

MARCO

(*Pauses, tone changes. Speaks deliberately and thoughtfully*) My mom knows I'm an atheist. She's not. She's Catholic, but real casually because that's how she was brought up. My mom's tolerant. She's real tolerant. She understands that there are things that she doesn't understand. (*Pause*) I was in AA for a few years and it's a very cultist kind of mentality. They make you surrender to a higher power and all that . . . . Nothing wrong with it. I played along. My dad, his brain is so fried, I don't know what he thinks. I don't know if you've ever seen *Cape Fear* with Robert De Niro. I would do that scene for my dad, "I'm as big as God and God is as small as I." And my dad would get so pissed off, he's like, "Marco, don't fucking say that about God." That kind of, like God is an actual person, he's listening. But I would do it to fuck with him. Things like that, you know what I mean, it's very traditional. I don't know what he would feel about Islam or anything like that or other religions. It's real live and let live.

News slide of women in burkinis coming out of the water fades in and voice over begins.[33]

SLIDE / VOICE OVER

Narrator: The French State Council, the country's supreme court, ruled the burkini ban, a ban on bathing suits that cover all of a woman except her face, hands, and feet, cannot be enforced legally. More than a dozen French seaside towns have chosen to ban the burkini after a string of terror attacks in France this summer.

13. WOMEN

Title slide fades in.
Ana and Heather are together;
Myra, Ellen, and Karen are together;
Saleem and Pastor Bill are standing separate from one another and
speak to the audience, rather than to each other.

ANA

I've definitely read stuff about like how the hijab's empowering. Like you don't have to do your hair. You don't have to do your makeup. You can be yourself. Some people feel more like safe.

ELLEN

Whenever you get to know people personally, then you see and you don't sort of have this monolithic idea. I came to have an understanding of modesty as a feminist act . . . . I don't want to belittle the very misogynist parts of Islam because that happens in any religion.

HEATHER

The best way that I've heard it put is, it privatizes a woman's sexuality. A woman can be who she is and be successful without having to have her sexuality on display. By saying you need to take off your hijab, that's saying you need to be forward with your sexuality or you're oppressed.

KAREN

(*Speaking up suddenly and angrily for the first time*) I have a completely different point of view about Muslims than what's being expressed here, so I tend not to talk about it because I sound like a crazed Trump person, which I'm totally not. I just feel like I come by my opinions honestly because I spent three years living in Pakistan dealing with Afghan refugees. My husband spoke fluent Urdu, so he could talk to all the Pakistanis and they would forget that he had a Western wife and they would talk very freely to him. Then he would tell me what they said when they thought no Westerners were listening. I can say that people who were highly educated Afghans were horrible people when they were speaking privately. They were *horrible* people. Towards women, towards Jews, towards Westerners, towards each other.

PASTOR BILL

That's the teaching of Muhammad. He puts women almost lower than he puts Jews.

KAREN

In some larger, nicer sense it wasn't their fault. It's the way they were raised. But their culture sucked, and their treatment of women . . . . Their only function was to have children. That's how they viewed women. And if anything, the least little thing went wrong, they would just kill them with complete impunity, and were honored for it. We saw it every day. A woman was bitten by a rabid dog. Her husband took her to the clinic. My husband is there. There were no female vaccinators available. These women are completely covered. Because it would be a male vaccinator, they just left. My husband said, "She's going to get rabies."

HEATHER

What we don't see is how oppressed women in the west are. When I grew up, I had an eating disorder, I had all sorts of things that, I think, women often get because we're forced to obsess about our bodies. That can be deadly.

SALEEM

My wife, you know didn't wear hijab, then she wore it, then she took it off . . . . I never saw it as the defining feature of a woman's faith.

KHADIJAH

We're not treated as normal citizens. Some companies put us in their ads here and there or have pictures of us at the mall or something, like [in] a hijab or whatever. We're still not normalized as any other citizen that just wears a headscarf. We are just not there yet.

News slide of men grieving the deaths of a cleric
and his associate fades in and voice over begins.[34]

SLIDE / VOICE OVER

Narrator: August 2016. A Muslim cleric and an associate were walking together following afternoon prayers at a mosque in the New York City borough of Queens when a gunman approached them from behind and shot both in the head at close range.

14. SAFE SPACE

Title slide fades in.
Khadijah and Lucy are in the center of the stage talking to each other.

LUCY

I feel like there's not a 100% safe space anywhere.

KHADIJAH

I'm actually more aware that I'm the only one who's Muslim in the room and that somebody might try to do something. I feel like people—like Donald Trump and the people who support him and the people he's bringing out of the woods now, because he's able to say this on national TV and then in huge groups of people—now people feel okay saying stuff.

LUCY

It's bad. I don't feel safe around white people. Just immediately, like immediately if I even get a tone that they might be not chill, I'm scared of them. I'm like oh man they're going to say something racist.

KHADIJAH

Oh yeah. The thing with hostility is as a Muslim, you can't even give them 2% of what they give you because you are going to come off like a terrorist, so if they tell you like, "Oh, you crazy Muslim," if you tell them, "Oh, you crazy racist white person," immediately they're going to say, "You see? We told you guys they're crazy."

News slide of ISIS bombing of a Baghdad shopping
center fades in as narrator begins.[35]

SLIDE / VOICE OVER

Narrator: Summer 2016. The Islamic State—also known as ISIL or ISIS or Daesh—bombs Baghdad, Iraq, killing nearly 300 people in the deadliest single car bombing in Baghdad since the 2003 Iraq War.

15. ISIS IS DAESH

Title slide fades in.
Aliyah and Aden are standing together.

ALIYAH

Daesh is a terrorist organization.

ADEN

They are not Muslim really. There is nothing in the Islamic religion make people kill each other.

ALIYAH

My name is Aliyah, and this is my husband Aden . . . . We are from Baghdad.

ADEN

I'm writing my thesis in political science. PhD. It's about Arab conflict in Iraq and how it affects Arab communities with neighboring countries like Iran and Turkey.

ALIYAH

I was teaching. I retired because circumstances is not well. They threaten the professors and they threatened all the teachers and the university. I didn't feel comfortable, really, the last years.

ADEN

Daesh . . . . They burned the libraries, they ruined the museum, the university. They prevent womans from going to study. But they make people join together to fight them. Now they are fighting them in Salah ad Din and Fallujah and all these spots. Now they pushing them out of the cities, every day. We hope that in six months that Daesh will be out of the country.

ALIYAH

They are very . . . savages really.

ADEN

Savages, they are savages, yes.

ALIYAH

They are hated by all.

ADEN

They are not Islam, not the ideas of Islam at all.

News slide of man holding a dead child fades in and voice over begins.

SLIDE / VOICE OVER

Narrator: An estimated 5,000+ people have drowned in the Mediterranean Sea in 2016 while seeking refuge from Syria's civil war. Clinton says,

(Clinton audio): "We're facing the worst refugee crisis since the end of World War II and I think the United States has to do more."

Narrator: Trump tells a cheering crowd,

(Trump audio): "I'm putting the people on notice that are coming here from Syria as part of this mass migration, that if I win, if I win, they're going back." [36]

16. REFUGEES AND IMMIGRANTS

Title slide fades in.
Myra, Ellen, and Karen are sitting together.
Saleem, Jay, Patrick, and Ana are also sitting.

JAY

If you have terrorists coming in, and you're trying to . . . . You're just asking people, interviewing people. You don't even have to be honest. There's a principle of Islam that says, "It's okay to even deny your faith if it's going to further the cause of Islam." That's a little frightening. We don't have a problem with you wanting to be here, but if ultimately your goal is to change the American legal system and the way we rule ourselves, then we do have a problem.

ELLEN

(*Looking at Jay*) It says in the Quran that [Muslims] must follow the law of the land. Our land is the Constitution, so [that's] insulting!

PATRICK

You can't figure them out. (Pause) The forty virgins thing sounded pretty cool but it's kind of like, I'll pass on all that.

ANA

(*Arguing with Patrick*) These people are displaced. They have to give up everything. They're not getting the jobs that people think they're getting, like, "Oh, they can just go to Walmart and get a job." Look, it's not that simple.

PATRICK

We have nothing to do with those people. Yeah, we're buying oil from them, but we don't share their politics. We don't share their religion. They need to leave us alone. Why do they want to come over here and bomb us and kill people over here? It makes no sense. Those people, they've been doing that for centuries over there. They're used to it.

ANA

(*To audience*) There are some people in my family that—while they don't agree 100% with Donald Trump— there's certain things that they are in agreeance with, which is very frustrating, especially since my parents are immigrants. To hear someone in your family say, "Yeah, we should increase our immigration laws and be stricter, kick the Mexicans out." I'm like, "That's us."

KAREN

We had people who—I don't want to call them friends but we spent time with them—who were in blood feuds, which meant they killed other people. (*Pause*) And then they would get visas to the U.S. and settle in the U.S. because they didn't want to be killed in their turn. These were people we would go over and watch TV with. Then I found out later why he emigrated to the U.S. and I was shocked. He had murdered all these people! I said, "Well, does his wife know about it?" And my husband said, "Know about it? She's proud of him!"

ELLEN

(*Frustrated, Ellen stands up and turns to Karen.*) I work with refugees all the time. I have never once had a problem with anybody, never once. (*Pauses, turns to audience*) One of the Afghan refugees . . . . He was so upset and so scared. This man has been a translator for the U.S. military for 10 years, so his family had been targeted. They had gotten him out of Afghanistan and into the United States. He went to Walmart and he got a pressure cooker. Somebody reported him there for buying a pressure cooker. They heard him talking to his friend in line at Walmart in a different language. They knew it was Middle Eastern or something. It was not Arabic but was Pashto or Dari. The FBI was alerted, and they started following him. They went to his house when he was gone. Only his wife, who didn't speak English, was there with the children. It scared her to death. It took, I don't know how many times. This is like, you're terrorizing him, *and* he was being terrorized in his *own* country. Finally, the U.S. military person, people that he translated for, had to go to their commander and have the commander talk to the FBI and say there is nothing wrong with this man. (*Pause*) He said, "Why, why did they do that, why? Because I bought a pressure cooker? What is wrong with the pressure cooker?"

A moment's pause.
Focus shifts to Saleem and Jay, who walk to the front, standing apart but both centered.

SALEEM

(*Speaks directly to the audience*) What's weird is sometimes I like, I wish I was just treated like nobody, like I'm a nobody. Does that make sense? You know, there's a luxury in being, in being no one. I feel like I'm talking like "Game of Thrones," I'm no one. Well when you, when you stick out . . . . Sometimes it's nice to be an ambassador, because you get to control the message. But sometimes it's also nice—you get tired of being an ambassador, you get tired of being like this professional Muslim, you wanna just be . . . . I get tired of having to represent my people.

JAY

(*Walks to center stage, pauses, and speaks boldly to audience.*) This election has not changed my ideas or values per se, but it has empowered me, thanks to Trump.

17. HUMANS

Title slide fades in.
Chris is on stage by himself.

CHRIS

We get to where we're going and there's gunfire going off, and as soon as I open that fucking door, dude, the dude jumps out. I take the shit off his head, and he sees his dad. His dad is like from here to the end of the block. These are grown ass men, dude. The dude is like 33, 34 years old, the dad is in his 60s, old man, and he just starts running. Boom, starts going, and he just starts going. I'm running after him. Shit's popping off, and he just had no fucking clue, didn't care about nothing at all, but his dad. His dad saw him and he gives this cry out and gives him another cry back out, and they're both just running. Man, if I could fucking paint the picture. I can see it I tasted the dirt, the sand, the fucking smells, the gunfire. The father grabs him by the fucking face, dude, grabs him on the side of the cheeks and just looks him in the eyes and just kisses him in the mouth. Not like a homo kiss, like this is his fucking son. He just kisses him so passionately, dude, tells him he loves him. Says he loves him and then pulls him to the side and he looks at me, and by then I've caught up to him. They're huffing and puffing and just wondering what the fuck I just did. I got me and another guy with me. The dad looks at me and kind of pushes his son aside. He just gives me a big old fucking kiss, dude, and then we both just start crying, dude. Tears coming out like, not the just got my ass kicked cry, but it was just like these tears of joy just come down the side of my mouth. He tells me, "Thank you, thank you, thank you." Right there, at that point, and I was at the beginning of one of my tours at that point, it was like, it's human. They're fucking human, period. All you motherfuckers, when we had them in custody, wanted to show them pornography or feed him pork, or slap him, or doing something stupid to him. I put myself in harm's way, I went through a lot. Fuck all y'all. They're fucking human.

Chris turns to leave the stage as the news slide of Donald Trump comes up and voice over begins.[37]
Chris looks up at the image of Donald Trump and stops, continuing to look at the screen.
As the voice over continues, the rest of the cast moves onto the stage, looking at the screen, with their backs to the audience.

SLIDE / VOICE OVER

Narrator: November 9, 2016. Surprising pundits and pollsters, Donald J. Trump wins Pennsylvania by 44,292 votes. He beats Secretary Clinton in Wisconsin by 22,748 votes. His victory in Michigan is by 10,704 votes. Nationally, Trump wins 45.9 percent of the popular vote and 306 of the Electoral College votes. Hillary Rodham Clinton wins 48 percent of the popular vote and 232 of the Electoral College votes. President-elect Trump vows to "Make America Great Again."

Lights fade to black.

Part II

Understanding *To Be Honest*

CHAPTER ONE

FROM PRIVATE SPACE TO PUBLIC SPHERE: *TO BE HONEST* IN PRODUCTION

Stacey Connelly

A ugusto Boal, the eminent stage director and founder of Theater of the Oppressed, a genre of Applied Theater dedicated to social justice, declared that, "It is not the place of the theater to show the correct path, but only to offer the means by which all possible paths may be examined".[38] The various paths that led to the premiere of *To Be Honest* emerged out of a serendipitous, collaborative, near-textbook example of transdisciplinary teaching, research, and artistic exploration. Indeed the play—its origin story, its source material, its connection to local, national, and global concerns—seemed the very definition of transdisciplinary creation, the alchemy that occurs when scholars from different disciplines train their focus on an issue and combine their varied approaches and methodologies. My contribution as director added another approach, another mode of working toward the same goal. To be clear, our collaborative process was not "interdisciplinary": an interdisciplinary model demonstrates how different fields of study can "talk to" each other, but transdisciplinary methods combine the perspectives and tools of various disciplines to address community, national, and even global problems.[39] To that end, my colleagues Sarah Beth Kaufman, William Christ, and Habiba Noor—scholars deeply engaged in social justice—not only combined their perspectives, but took their tools far beyond the classroom. With their team of student researchers, they spent weeks interviewing San Antonians of various ethnicities and backgrounds: civilian and military, poor and affluent, religious and secular, conservative and liberal, gay and straight. Their data yielded fascinating analysis, experiential curricula, and a number of scholarly publications, but also—to my surprise—an artistic impulse inspired in part from a unit I led the previous year about Epic Theater and documentary drama.

In October 2016, Drs. Noor and Kaufman invited me for coffee and handed me what looked like a script, explaining that the text was taken from transcribed interviews they had conducted over the summer with a cross-section of San Antonians. It reminded them, they said, of *The Laramie Project*, a play I had introduced in the course we team-taught, First Year Experience: Social Justice. A documentary drama drawn from interviews with the residents of Laramie, Wyoming, *The Laramie Project* explored the effects of a hate crime, the murder of a gay college student, Matthew Shepard, on a close-knit community. The script in my hand, however, dealt with an entirely different event, one that had yet to happen: the upcoming presidential election. Could this material, they asked, become a play, too? The best way to find out, I told them, was to have actors read it. They looked dismayed. "Aloud?" they asked. "But it isn't ready!" I assured them that it was not only ready, but overdue for a workshop, an essential step in play development. As potential playwrights, my colleagues needed to see and hear their drama performed—read by real people in front of a real audience—to find out if their text contained those elements that make a work dramatic: character, conflict, progression, and purpose. Happily, they agreed and thus began an artistic process that, through the authors' combined expertise, continued research, thoughtful revision, and theatrical imagination, condensed an overwhelming amount of data into a concise and compelling work of art.

Even in its earliest form, *To Be Honest* was deeply theatrical: it employed the dramatic convention of compressing time and space to create an environment of ideological opposites. Its structure, characters, and themes drew on traditions of political theater going back as far as the ancients—Greek choruses and narrative monologues—to techniques from the most up-to-date forms of documentary drama, combining historical events with modern media. Its presentational style hearkened back to the Epic Theater of Bertolt Brecht and Erwin Piscator, a style that rejected illusionism in favor of minimalist, constructivist sets and making the "fourth wall"—the invisible boundary between audience and actor—disappear. As a theater historian specializing in Interwar German drama, I was also reminded of the Weimar Republic's innovative *Zeittheater*, or dramas that staged narrative and eyewitness accounts of contemporary events, as well as the "Living Newspaper" productions that recreated recent history through montages of images, sound recordings, and film. My author-colleagues, much like Augusto Boal, employed interviews as part of their methodology: going into a community, asking questions, and exploring problems theatrically as a spur to political action. What struck me most, however, was the authors' creative use of those interviews, not just as source material, but as dialogue—an approach borrowed from the genre known as "verbatim theater," in which official transcripts of court proceedings or public inquiries serve as dramatic fodder, transforming the stage into philosopher and sociologist Jürgen Habermas's ideal of the "public sphere," a key component of a democratic society.

Some of these associations were apparent from the beginning; others arose through workshopping the play, a process of adaptation to assist the authors in "changing hats": transitioning from researchers to story-tellers, from analyzing to dramatizing. In adapting any non-dramatic literature for theatrical performance, the writers must find the motive and means to transform material intended for private consumption into an effective communal experience. What was it about their interviews with so many San Antonians that demanded a public setting, that would resonate with an audience outside of academia? What dramatic means could be employed to enact the narratives they had recorded, yet leave the simple power of storytelling intact? The authors recognized this tension—this necessary balance between personal anecdote and performative act; it was apparent in their working title, *Between Public and Private: Imagining and Experiencing Islam in San Antonio, 2016.*

To accelerate the move from narrative to dramatic mode, I prepared for the workshop. The shock of the November 2016 election—an event we were still trying to absorb—made a play about political rhetoric surrounding Islam, race, and immigration all the more urgent. I read and reread the text, a little unnerved by its long monologues and, by contemporary standards, an enormous number of roles. How would an audience remember all these characters? How did their monologues relate to each other? Would an audience be able to make the connections? Where was the script going and what was its goal? Amid all these questions, I gathered an ensemble, while the authors and I invited a discerning audience of fellow academics and artists. Our venue was Trinity's Attic Theater, a modest black-box space reserved for class meetings, student productions, and new play development.

For the cast, I recruited twenty-three players for twenty-three parts. From the beginning, it struck me as vital to cast one actor for each role, rather than double- and triple-cast, a practice common in professional theater for the sake of cost and efficiency. Yet the glory of the play was the variety of its characters, spanning four generations and virtually every demographic of San Antonio's population. Such specific roles required not just experienced actors, but individuals who represented the age and ethnicities of the project's diverse subjects. Fortunately, theater professors can commandeer performance classes, and universities offer an ideal casting pool. There were few difficulties in finding African Americans, Hispanics, South Asians—even Sikhs—among students, faculty, and alumni. To fill the roles of late middle-aged and elderly characters, I drew on San Antonio's small but vigorous theatrical community, including some professional actors, to embody the characters' unique identities.

Complicating the performance of these identities, however, was the notion of "character" itself: though the research subjects' identities were protected by invented names, the characters behind those names were real people. They were not "characters" at all, in fact—not in the traditional sense of fictional constructs, or even figures "based on a true story." Rather, they were entities who, at this stage of the process, existed only in their transcribed words, a circumstance that threw into relief the primacy of those words and the actors' obligation to deliver them with accuracy. What kind of approach, then, might best allow an actor to create a role, yet also remind their audience that the character they embodied was an actual person? I wondered how an actor could treat the text so that the words they spoke defined their character with utter clarity, but also underscored the mystery of their real identity. The principle of anonymity was central to the project's integrity as a document and its impact as a work of art.

The play's contrasting mix of characters seemed an imaginative take on the "risks and rewards of diversity" trope, in which a polyglot assortment of mysterious characters thickens the plots of classic "whodunits" or caper movies like *Stalag 17* and *Ocean's Eleven*. In that spirit of adventure, and as a director who adores the *Rashomon*-like replay of multiple perspectives, I couldn't help asking, "What would happen if all these opinionated people, of such different ethnicities and religious traditions, were locked in a room and compelled to communicate?" The script reminded me of the public television series from the 1970s *Meeting of Minds*, in which historical personages from different eras sat down for a lively discussion of a contemporary topic, informed by their wildly differing world views. Classes in acting and improvisation employ similar scenarios to help actors identify with their characters' perspectives and develop interesting conflicts. The ironic difference with *To Be Honest*, though, is that, despite living in the same time and place, its characters, divided by barriers of race, class, and politics, would likely never meet nor identify with people who were vastly different; some, based on their comments, clearly feared interaction—much less a serious conversation—with those of other ethnicities, religions, or polit-ical convictions. Yet if these characters could coexist for an hour, what would they say? Who would talk to whom? Who would pick a quarrel and who would find a kindred spirit? What kind of ideological clashes, surprising similarities, and productive collisions might occur if San Antonio's citizens were willing to compare ideas about race, religion, and politics?

My fascination with the simple idea of sitting down for a conversation led me, for the workshop perfor-mance, to avoid the traditional components of staging—a ground plan, blocking, and pictorial composition. Instead, actors sat in an arc of chairs that spanned the stage, a configuration offering a complete view of the characters. No entrances and exits took place. When not speaking, characters still participated as listeners and witnesses, aware of each other's presence. It was an approach we would return to—this ever-present, full-cast image—as the script, design, and staging evolved in subsequent productions. For the workshop performance, though, this up-close arrangement of actors and audience—face-to-face, with nothing separating them except a few feet of empty stage, meant that some aesthetic distance was in order. Despite our presentation of factual material, we still needed to inspire what poet and critic Samuel Taylor Coleridge famously termed "that willing suspension of disbelief," the convention that the spectator accepts as true the artificial world presented on stage.[40] Our "world" was far from artificial, but it still required our audience to accept the fiction that the theater, a public environment, was actually its opposite, a private space, so that the characters' willingness to share such personal information seemed plausible.

We created that space through the use of the invisible "fourth wall," with actors directing their attention not to the audience, but to an interviewer. Even seated together as a focus group, characters still told their stories to the unseen interviewer, placed downstage of the scenes in the direction of the audience. In the first three iterations of *To Be Honest*, the interviewer began as an actual character, played by a young actor to suggest the role of a student researcher. After thanking her subjects and assuring their anonymity, she posed the question that launches the play, "A lot has been said about Islam in this election. What have you heard?" Once the first character began to respond, the interviewer exited discreetly, while the characters behaved as if she were still there. By the fourth iteration of *To Be Honest*, the physical character disappeared, replaced with projections introducing the project, its intent, and the question; the interviewer's presence, however, remained throughout, in the characters' placement and focus. As the engine for so much truth and passion, the interviewer's authority and intention make the world of the play credible.

With some basic decisions made about casting, staging, and style, my part of the workshop was ready, so with the actors and a small audience that early December evening, we began our experiment. For the first time, the authors heard the words they'd pored over as scholars uttered in a theatrical context, the words expressing intimate thoughts entrusted to them by their research subjects, now exposed and animated by actors in a performative setting. It's an unforgettable moment, when the mode of performance turns private words public: suddenly, individual histories become collective experience, personal opinions evolve into discourse, and the simplest act takes on symbolic freight. The act of performance thus captured both worlds, an intimate realm of memory and experience and an open forum of active exchange—Habermas's public sphere, where all citizens' voices are heard regarding issues of local, national, or even global import.

The birth of *To Be Honest* meets what Habermas determines as three preconditions for emergence of a public sphere: disregard of status, a domain of common concern, and inclusivity.[41] In a city as racially and economically divided as San Antonio, inclusivity and disregard of status are hard to achieve; but suddenly, through the medium of theater, every person on stage was eligible, equal, and invited to contribute. Like the influential eighteenth-century salons, *Tischgesellschaften* ("table societies"), and coffeehouses that Habermas describes in *The Structural Transformation of the Public Sphere*, the research project-turned-play became a twenty-first century salon that put all participants on the same level, regardless of their cultural, educational, or financial status. As Habermas describes this phenomenon of social integration, " . . . in the *salons* of the fashionable ladies, noble as well as bourgeois, sons of princes and counts associated with sons of watchmakers and shopkeepers. In the *salon*, the mind was no longer in the service of a patron; 'opinion' became emancipated from the bonds of economic dependence."[42] In the same way, *To Be Honest* offered a site of free exchange, removing the barriers of income, language, and San Antonio's toxic legacy of real estate "covenants" that enforced segregation in housing and business development—city planning that divided the city into sixteen school districts and discouraged its diverse residents from social interaction, much less serious discussion about contentious issues of race and class. The reactions of that first audience—and audiences since—have made it clear that the play's forthrightness about race, religion, and politics was a bracing experience, and that, for many, it was the first time they had heard such frank and startling opinions from members of their own community, despite sharing the same corner of South Texas for decades.

Like the denizens of Habermas's Enlightenment-era coffeehouse, the characters of *To Be Honest* gather to investigate and testify about a "domain of common concern,"[43] turning their salon—in this case, the stage—into a tribunal. Since the age of Aeschylus and his *Oresteia*, theatrical production has served its audience as a concentrated court of public opinion. Issues are interrogated and characters debate as fiercely as prosecutors and defenders, with the audience as jury and judge. It's an intimidating prospect, this judgment, yet for most playwrights, what at first seems the most fearful aspect of a workshop—audience reaction—turns out to be the catalyst that moves the play from page to stage. Such was the case with our workshop production; the spectators' warmth and involvement in the performance gave life to the characters' testimony. In the discussion afterward, observers and performers responded with enthusiasm, curiosity, and useful suggestions. For the authors, the workshop allowed them to watch and listen, ask questions, and consider changes. By the end of the evening, my colleagues realized they had achieved something significant: from hundreds of hours of recordings and reams of transcriptions, they had distilled the personal experience of their subjects into a dramatic event presenting vital issues for public discussion. Their completed first draft was not only stage-worthy, but moving, thoughtful, timely, and urgent.

The playwrights' subsequent revisions of *To Be Honest* embraced the presentational style of the Living News-paper, an agitation-propaganda genre, performed by traveling Soviet troupes to educate citizens about current events and government programs. Taken up by stage director Erwin Piscator in Weimar Germany, the Living Newspaper gained prominence in reaction to WWI, reflecting popular backlash against militarism, capitalism, and bourgeois entertainment. Part of an artistic movement known as *Die Neue Sachlichkeit* (The New Objectivity), Piscator's *Zeittheater* rejected the realistic conventions of illusionism for a self-consciously theatrical style that exposed the apparatus of the theater, its stage equipment and machinery, to portray the hidden machinations of public figures and political parties.[44] Such non-realistic devices functioned as what Brecht would later call *Verfremdungseffekten*, or "distancing effects," intended to blunt emotional identification with the characters and remind audiences that they were not in some imaginary space, but in a theater, watching a play, and should therefore avoid the "hypnosis" of psychological realism that paralyzes the spectator and precludes action. Rather, in true Epic fashion, the audience should focus on the big picture, intellectually engaging with the play's ideas, and analyzing its action against a larger backdrop of national events or global trends.

For the same reasons, eager for a new, modern production style that demonstrated the power of science and industry in contemporary life, Piscator made liberal use of what was then cutting-edge technology—recordings, projections, radio, and film—techniques that portrayed the world with documentary-like accuracy and later influenced the inventive productions of the U.S. Federal Theater Project (FTP), an arm of the Works Progress Administration during the New Deal era of the 1930s.[45] With titles like *One Third of a Nation, Triple-A Plowed Under*, and *It Can't Happen Here*, the FTP's Living Newspapers addressed issues ranging from poverty and housing to fascism and farming. Combining the arts of theater, rhetoric, and cinema with journalism and social science-based research, these quasi-documentaries connected fictional scenes with recent events, accompanied by projected facts, statistics, and newsreels. Since the heyday of this genre during the Great Depression, countless productions have employed these same Epic Theater devices, staging reenactments of historical or current events alongside actual news footage as a backdrop, contrast, and complement to their plots, reflecting their era's anxieties, inequities, and political battles.

Similarly, as shown in co-author William Christ's artful design of projections, sound recordings, and television news stories, *To Be Honest* captured the fraught atmosphere of the months preceding the 2016 election. As transitions between the episodes, Christ's audio-visual score of projections, sound effects, news reports, and campaign soundbites presented signal moments in local, national, and international news that informed the increasingly hostile tone of campaign rhetoric and the tense, fearful reactions of the characters as they experienced the impact of the Muslim ban, hate crimes, mass shootings, bombings, and the global refugee crisis. An example of Brecht's Epic *Verfremdungseffekt*, these brief news flashes shift the viewer's perspective from the intimate lives of the characters to the broader realm of public life, tracking events that portray the devastation wrought by the Afghanistan and Iraq wars, and the ever-growing violence stoked by extremism, Islamophobia, and politicians who conflate Islam and terrorism.

These intermittent shifts of focus invite comparison and analysis of how personal lives, political events, and public discourse are related. Beginning with a recording of the raucous campaign rally when Trump called for a Muslim ban, successive transitions show how the intolerance of global leaders trickles down to national, state, and even local levels: in one news item, San Antonio televangelist pastor John Hagee inveighs against immigrants; in the transition before Episode 5, Texas Senator Ted Cruz accuses the Obama administration of ignoring "radical Islamic terrorism." Demonizing of Muslims and immigrants is also exposed on a global scale in one of the play's transitions that reports the U.S. bombing of Syria and Iraq, and another that features the now-famous photo of a rescue worker cradling the body of three-year-old Alan Kurdi, a Syrian boy who drowned in the Mediterranean along with other members of his family fleeing the war. This tragic image makes clear the connection between the prejudice and violence that drive citizens from their countries and the fates of thousands of refugees turned away by hostile nations.

Two transitions in particular draw a dramatic contrast between events that caused Islam to be blamed for extremist violence and events experienced by the Muslims who appear in the scenes that follow. In Episode 8, a character called Khadijah, a Muslim woman, speaks after a newsflash of the Pulse nightclub massacre in Orlando. Expressing her horror at the mass shooting and her fear of being targeted as a Muslim, she tells of a gay man confronting her in public—not out of prejudice, but a desire to say that he has nothing against her. The impact of that moment, of encountering kindness instead of retaliation, is tremendous. Similarly, following the transition about the lives lost in the bombing of Baghdad by ISIS in Episode 15, an Iraqi couple who fled the war decry the violence of ISIS, calling them "savages" and declaring that "They [ISIS] are not Islam. Not the idea of Islam at all." In ironic opposition to these glimmers of hope, a news transition before Episode 9 that announces a fatwa signed by 70,000 Muslim clerics against global terrorist organizations is followed by a character called Jay, a retired Lieutenant Colonel, whose first words proclaim, "They're here to take over the country, the radical Islamists."

As part of the transitions, all episodes were preceded by projected titles, another example of a distancing effect that contributes to, in the words of Bertolt Brecht, the "literarization of the theater," shifting focus from characters and plot to the play's words and ideas.[46] Each title, usually an evocative word or phrase spoken by a character in the scene, not only hints at the episode's subject, but alludes to its theme. Such forecasting of the topic grants spectators the privilege of foreknowledge, but also raises questions, building anticipation about the title's meaning within the scene and the larger realm of the play. As the scene plays out, spectators feel the pleasure of not just recognizing the title word or phrase, but of understanding its context. Literalization through the use of projected titles achieves what Brecht described as "complex seeing," because ". . . it is more important to think above the stream than to think in the stream."[47] In other words, the simultaneous acts of reading a projection, hearing a recording, seeing an image, and watching an actor—especially when those points of attention contrast or conflict—allow comprehension of a play on multiple levels.

While its use of technology and political themes borrows from the tradition of Epic Theater, *To Be Honest* diverges from Epic style in its more rigorous approach to text. Drawn solely from interviews with residents of San Antonio, the text of *To Be Honest* gives the play an immediacy and authenticity unmatched by other nonfiction genres. Generally known as "verbatim theater," this dramatic form, taken from official testimony and government records, began with Peter Weiss's *The Investigation* (1963), an exposé of the Frankfurt trials, culled from two years of witness testimony about the atrocities at Auschwitz.[48] Miscarriages of justice, in fact, are the most frequent targets of verbatim dramas: Eric Bentley's *Are You Now or Have You Ever Been?* (1972)[49] condensed years of House Un-American Activities Committee (HUAC) hearings into a taut drama about the persecution of theater and film artists, while *The Chicago Conspiracy Trial* (1979) by Frank Condon and Ron Sossi[50] includes a cast of 36 and used trial transcripts to interrogate the U.S. justice system and reveal violations of the defendants' civil rights that, on appeal, overturned the results of that proceeding. With its long tradition of dramas known as "Tribunal Plays," Tricycle Theater of Kilburn, North London, has staged verbatim reconstructions of public inquiries, beginning with *Half the Picture: The Scott Arms to Iraq Inquiry* (1994), a play by Richard Norton-Taylor and John McGrath about the Thatcher government's sale of arms to Iraq. As noted by theater historian David Lane, Tricycle's premiere of *Half the Picture* "was condensed from 400 hours of evidence given at the Scott Inquiry" and "presented as a reconstruction of the trial itself."[51] Over the next fifteen years, Tricycle produced eight more verbatim plays, among them *Srebrenica—the U.N. 61 Ruling* (1996), *The Stephen Lawrence Inquiry—The Colour of Justice* (1999), and *Bloody Sunday: Scenes from the Saville Inquiry* (2006).

As Lane observes, verbatim theater resists categorization because the kind of material portrayed and the methods of collecting it can differ widely, depending on the subject:

> The manner by which that material is gathered and how it is framed in performance is what varies. It may be garnered from face-to-face discussions with the writer or actor, written testimonies, transcriptions of court hearings and print journalism or recordings of interviews and news reports. It could then be structured as a tribunal reconstruction, a fluid collage of written and spoken statements and interviews, a combination of statements and fictional scenes based on evidence, or even a mixture of interpretive dance and text as with the dance company DV8's *To Be Straight With You* (2008) which explored homophobia in a liberal, multicultural and multi-faith Britain.[52]

Yet no matter its topic, setting, or technique of gathering written or spoken material, verbatim theater reveals the conflicting sides at the heart of an issue and what's at stake for those involved. Its frequent focus on public testimony as a form of investigation depicts conflict as inherent to the process, presenting opposing forces in ideological contest and a pitched battle for justice.

Hence, during the period of revision before the play's premiere, I wondered how the authors might arrange their subjects' individual and unrelated accounts so that characters could still connect, if not in time and space, then thematically. More important, how would isolated characters generate conflict, an essential component of the drama? Fortunately, the authors had conducted interviews in various configurations: alone, in pairs, and in focus groups, which they skillfully exploited for dramatic purposes, giving characters both private moments and opportunities for dialogue. For example, Episode 3, "Millennials," featured a focus group of characters called Heather, Doug, Ana, and Marco, who find common ground in their discussion of popular culture and social media. Meanwhile, another focus group comprised of senior citizen characters called Myra, Ellen, and Karen, discover shared attitudes as well, but also significant differences. These new scenes, among other conversations in groups of twos and threes, allowed characters to report conflicts about politics, race, and religion and clash directly about various issues. Conflict even arose in the monologues: Chris, an Iraq War veteran, shares memories that are deeply confessional; his conflict is internal and private, an effective illustration of the single-person interview in uncovering truths that might not occur in a focus-group setting. Episode 12, "Erased," featured eight characters of different religions and ethnicities—Joshua, Heather, Pastor Bill, Lucy, Donny, Jay, Marco, and Saleem—in what seems an intense exchange of competing ideas. The artful division and arrangement of their comments, culled from separate interviews, put the characters in a parallel conversation, reminiscent of speakers at a town hall or public inquiry.

In discussion with the authors, I got approval to continue with the large cast and readers theater approach that accompanied our first reading. On a practical level, given the large cast and limited rehearsals, it seemed unwise to expect memorized performances of long monologues with so little rehearsal time. Stylistically, we liked the distancing effect of actors holding scripts as a reminder to audiences that the players did not embody fictional characters, but real people, channeling their thoughts and experiences from the text they held in their hands. I was thrilled that the authors retained the play's remarkable origins as introductory information, and that the long and powerful narrative of the soldier, Chris, had been separated into distinct episodes marking key events and changes in perspective. His role as a soldier in the "War on Terror"—in direct, deadly conflict with Muslims—reified the bigotry and distrust that other non-Muslim characters in *To Be Honest* discussed in the abstract. Chris's scenes alternated with group scenes, making him the only character with his own episodes, and the only one whose story is told in continuing segments rather than snapshots. His character arc, transforming from a violent, angry private driven by prejudice to a compassionate protector of a Muslim civilian, unified the play and provided its satisfying conclusion.

With titles like "Political Correctness," "Refugees and Immigrants," "ISIS is Daesh," and "Orlando," the more compact, revised scenes tracked closely with the unfolding of key state, national, and global events leading to election day. An essential addition was the projection of those events, narrated as news stories, on a large screen that, outside of a few folding chairs, offered the play's only "scenery," showing news clips followed by scene titles, connecting the microcosm of San Antonio with the macrocosm of the nation. The words and image of local megachurch pastor John Hagee echoed the Islamophobia expressed by Texas Senator Ted Cruz in the video that followed. Informing subsequent scenes were news clips showing attacks on Sikhs and Muslim clerics, the Orlando massacre, and bombings in Baghdad, juxtaposed with horrifying news about the refugee crisis. The most striking images came from the ominous videos that opened and closed the play: after the opening blackout, Donald Trump appeared at a rally, promising his Muslim ban; the closing video declared his victory, ending with "President-Elect Trump vows to make America great again." Directly following, the playwrights' inclusion of a rapid vocal montage of key statements from individual characters provided the perfect transition and introduction to the large cast, with their chorus-like expression of the passions and anxiety evoked by Trump's inflammatory rhetoric.

As *To Be Honest* evolved, so did my direction and the characters' focus. The narrative form of the play itself, combined with certain characters' passion and eloquence, made some of the longer monologues sound like poetry; staged in isolation and presented by strong actors only heightened the theatricality of delivery. Khadijah's haunted reaction to the massacre in Orlando, Joshua's recounting of his conversion to Islam, and Jay's disturbing conviction that Islam was a religion of violence rose to the level of classical soliloquies. Most dramatic of all was Chris, whose final words not only concluded the play, but were meant as admonitions for all to hear: a demand for tolerance and belief in our common humanity. After the second workshop performance in May 2016, it was clear that these speeches resonated with our audience; the characters who spoke them captured so intensely the play's themes of unity and tolerance that the fourth wall—the invisible barrier between actor and audience—would have to be dismantled for these episodes. The public dimension of these speeches—impassioned opinions that spoke to policy, government, morality, and humanity—demanded direct communication with the audience.

A later performance of *To Be Honest* at the Tobin Center in downtown San Antonio returned to our workshop production's original ground plan of the entire cast seated in an arc across the back of the stage. When it was time to play their scenes, actors walked downstage to stand or sit in various arrangements, but always returned to their upstage chairs as witnesses and participants. Inspired by the larger space and the reality of Trump's promises that had now come true, we tried a new composition: at the opening and closing videos that bookended Trump's campaign and eventual triumph, the actors rose from their arc and gathered downstage, shoulder to shoulder, in a tight group, backs to the audience, eyes lifted to the events on screen. For me, that formation was the most affecting, an expression of unity that moved me as much as the characters' diversity. Gathered together, they looked large and impressive, but under that giant image of President Trump against an American flag, also vulnerable and small. When the video ended, they turned around, facing the audience. All citizens, all San Antonians, witnessing events of magnitude that would affect millions of lives and define an era for years to come.

The sobering conclusion of *To Be Honest* brings us back to this chapter's introduction of our project's inception and its transdisciplinary goals of solving local, national, and even global problems. While we cannot claim victory over the global scourge of Islamophobia, we can certainly say, based on audience response, that we raised awareness about the marginalized groups within our community. We learned much, in fact, about the impact of our production. In the transdisciplinary spirit, the playwrights designed interactive formats for the roundtable discussions that took place after the performance. Audience members got refreshments and sat down to talk with strangers about topics that most of us were taught not to discuss: politics and religion. Like the interview subjects who inspired the play, our audience, too, was given permission *to be honest*, and their written and spoken responses were frank, remarkable, and vulnerable. What impressed me most, however, about the discussions was the participants' active listening. Our invaluable partnership with Texas Public Radio's "Dare to Listen" campaign provided us not only with marketing assistance, but also framed our production and post-show talk-backs as reflective of their own program's goals of civil discourse and a chance to hear new voices.

Working with admired colleagues is always a pleasure, but the chance to collaborate as fellow artists on a complex long-term project was deeply rewarding. Watching the text evolve activated my own imagination and assisted me greatly in staging and actor coaching. Working with actors so diverse in age, experience, and ethnicity made me a better director, because I couldn't fall back on the pedagogic approach that generally works with college students. Our diverse cast brought rich life experience to the play and needed minimal instruction in how to animate their characters. My principal tasks were conceptual and technical—devising a unified style that ensured the actors could be seen and the text could be heard. Personally, *To Be Honest* compelled me to ask more questions—about my community, my politics, and my own beliefs and blind spots. The answers weren't always the ones I wanted, but there was value and freedom in the searching. I also developed new tools for staging readers theater, a performance genre that seems especially suited to verbatim productions.

It makes me proud that such a compelling dramatic work arose from a summer research project at a small liberal arts institution. I hope other campuses and community venues will take up *To Be Honest*, but my fervent wish is to see it produced at regional theaters in cities like Chicago, Houston, Seattle, Portland, Los Angeles, Atlanta, Minneapolis, Philadelphia, and Washington, D.C. For financial and artistic reasons, professional productions would likely discard the readers theater format in favor of a memorized, fully acted production peopled by a much smaller cast. While this downsized approach might not present the play's diversity to its best advantage, it would afford spectators the pleasure of watching eight actors inhabit twenty-two characters, transforming themselves to portray multiple identities and the common humanity that unites them all.

CHAPTER TWO

ALL THE NEWS . . .

William G. Christ

"Were it left to me to decide whether we should have a government without newspapers, or newspapers without a government, I should not hesitate a moment to prefer the latter. But I should mean that every man should receive those papers & be capable of reading them."[53]

THOMAS JEFFERSON

The months during which the interviews for *To Be Honest* were collected was a time of explosive news events.[54] During the summer of 2016, these events became fodder for national political discourse, with presidential candidates using the stories to help define their own positions and to attack each other.[55] Political candidates try to control and dominate the news narrative by promoting key elements of their agenda (e.g., immigration, jobs, trade, etc.), by framing stories in ways that support their own viewpoints (e.g., "Obstruction, Lies and Dishonor: Hillary's Benghazi Legacy"[56]), and by encouraging their supporters to evaluate them by the standards they have created for themselves (e.g., "Trump Says Players Who Don't Stand for Anthem 'Shouldn't Be in the Country'"[57]). The presidential campaign during the summer of 2016 was no different.

There were many events that took place during the 2016 presidential campaign that could have been included in the play. For example, we could have included the moments when Hillary Clinton and Donald Trump announced their candidacies in 2015, or the first time the FBI began an investigation of Clinton's use of a private email system. The news clips could have included more of the chilling events that helped define the campaigns and may have contributed to the outcome, including the June 2015 mass shooting during a prayer meeting at a historic Black church in Charleston, South Carolina that killed nine; or the December 2015 San Bernardino, California mass shooting at a holiday office party, during which fourteen were killed and twenty-two were wounded. Or, the play could have included the July 2016 attack on Bastille Day, when a truck was driven onto a sidewalk in Nice, France, killing at least eighty-four people and injuring hundreds more.

Just as journalists must choose which news stories to include in their newscasts, we also had to decide which stories to include in *To Be Honest*. We decided to limit news clips to events that took place between December 2015 and November 2016. Trump's December 2015 call for a complete, outright ban on all Muslims entering the country was historic and provided an ideal opening for the play. The play ends with the announcement that

Donald Trump is the president-elect. These two news events provide bookends for the narrative. Once selected, the news clips acted similarly to a newscast: they helped set the agenda for what was coming next, they framed important issues, and they helped prime the audience to think about how to evaluate politics and politicians.[58] This chapter explains the use of news clips in terms of agenda-setting, framing, and priming, before discussing how some of the interviewees used news events to frame their responses to questions.[59]

AGENDA-SETTING

In agenda-setting, the audience is not told what to think, but rather what to think about.[60] Of the twelve episodes in the play that used news clips, five set the agenda for the episode.

Congruent Messages: Episodes 6, 14, and 15

Several news clips "set up" episodes by presenting news that is highlighted or elaborated on in the episodes. Before Episode 6, "Sikhs" and 14, "Safe Space," what is salient in the news clips is that Sikhs and Muslims in the United States were attacked and even killed. We then learn in the episodes that the Sikh and Muslim characters in the play fear for their lives. Before Episode 15, "ISIS is Daesh," there is a news report of an attack by ISIS on Baghdad. The audience is asked to think about the fact that Muslim terrorists attack other Muslims. In the episode itself, we hear two Iraqi Muslims talk about how horrible ISIS is and that ISIS is not a group that follows Islam. The three news clips and episodes are congruent.[61]

 While the news clips cited above prepare the audience for what is discussed, other news clips present agendas that are interpreted differently, and even challenged, in the episodes.

Noncongruent Messages: Episodes 5 and 8

In Episode 5, "Political Correctness," the news reports that presidential candidate and U.S. Senator Ted Cruz convened a committee meeting on "Radical Islamic Terrorism," in which he claimed the "administration is willfully turning a blind eye to radical Islamic terrorism."[62] The news clip set the agenda for a robust discussion about political correctness.

 In the presidential campaign, political correctness was one of the many issues debated, specifically with President Obama's and, for a time, Hillary Clinton's unwillingness to use the words "radical Islam." Their reluctance to use the term was used to bludgeon Democrats. Republicans framed their rhetoric so that anyone who could not say "radical Islam" was considered weak on terrorists and terrorism. They primed audiences to think that using the term "radical Islam" was a measure of a candidate's strength and patriotism.

 In Episode 8, "Orlando," the news clip reminds the audience about the slayings at Pulse, a gay nightclub in Orlando, Florida.[63] The Orlando shooting was the worst terrorist attack in the United States since 9/11. In the episode, the audience hears different interpretations of the attack. From a Muslim character we hear, "I'm Khadijah. My first reaction to the Orlando shooting was, 'Oh my God. I hope it wasn't a Muslim.' When I heard it was a Muslim I was like, 'Oh no. Here we go. They're going to start harassing us again.'" Donny, a gay Republican character, confides unhappily, "The church I attend, after the Orlando massacre, the priest wanted to have members of the church to reach out to the Muslim community and dine with them. I had the opposite opinion.

They should reach out to us." And Ellen, a character who works with refugees, states, "The Muslim community, why should they be expected to defend themselves to Christians when we have hate crimes done in the name of Christianity in this country? Do we hear criticism of the Christian community when the Klan did that? The American Nazi Party defends their whole principles on religious grounds!"[64] The news clip set the agenda for the episode that followed; that is, the audience was encouraged to think about Orlando. Yet, the conversation that took place in the episode presented a variety of frames for interpreting the event.[65]

FRAMING AND PRIMING

Framing,[66] which proponents of agenda-setting theory call second-level agenda setting, "is based on the assumption that how an issue is characterized in news reports can have an influence on how it is understood by audiences."[67] Framing is about both how the news is presented and how audiences understand it. Of the twelve episodes preceded by news clips, seven provided frames for understanding how to think about what was coming next. Many of these frames are used to prime the audience about different issues.

The Introduction: Framing the Play

The play begins with Trump's call to ban all Muslims from entering the United States. "Donald J. Trump is calling for a total and complete shutdown of Muslims entering the United States until our country's representatives can figure out what the hell is going on . . . . We have no choice . . . WE HAVE NO CHOICE." After the video, the "Introduction" to the performance begins with the audience hearing different perceptions of Islam. The news clip shows Trump framing immigration as an issue in which true American's "have no choice." It is the intent of the authors to prime the audience to think about the candidates and themselves, in terms of their position toward Islam and Muslim refugees.[68]

Episode 7: A U.S. Soldier, Right?

The audio clip before Episode 7, "A U.S. Soldier, Right?" claims, "According to the Council on Foreign Relations, in 2016, the Obama administration dropped at least 26,171 bombs. This means that every day the U.S. military blasted combatants or civilians overseas with seventy-two bombs; that's three bombs every hour, twenty-four hours a day."[69] These chilling statistics position the U.S. as a powerful, destructive force. The slide that accompanies the audio clip shows a town in Syria during an intense Coalition bombing raid. The news story is a prelude to a monologue by the character Chris, a U.S. soldier who spent tours of combat duty in Iraq and Afghanistan and who was penalized by his superior officer for acknowledging that his unit was holding an innocent civilian. Together, both the news clip and episode frame U.S. actions as troubling.

Episode 9: Muslims Do Condemn Islamic Terrorism

In Episode 9, "Debating Islam," there are multiple views presented about Islam. One of the ideas we heard in our interviews was that Muslims did not speak out against terrorism perpetrated in the name of Islam. In the news clip before this episode, we learn that almost 70,000 Muslim clerics (religious leaders) meeting in India came together to pass a fatwa (a nonbinding authoritative legal opinion in Islamic law[70]) against global terrorist organizations.[71] This news clip primes the audience to realize that many Muslims *have* spoken out against global terrorists. This information and the episode that follows challenges audience members to reflect upon and possibly question their views.

Episode 10: Hope and Peace

Before Episode 10, "Hope and Peace," the news clip presents internationally recognized U.S. evangelical pastor John Hagee recommending that his followers vote for Donald Trump.[72] By showing Hagee promoting Trump, the audience is primed to think about the role of evangelical pastors and other religious leaders in promoting political agendas. If we believe Hagee's argument, then we are primed to see Trump as the only viable candidate. This clip comes just before the episode where characters identified as Evangelical Christians talk about Islam and suggests the idea that religion and politics are intertwined in this country.

Episode 12: Erased

In the news clip before Episode 12, "Erased," Muhammad Ali has just died and Senator Bernie Sanders uses Ali's death to remind Trump supporters that Ali was a devoted Muslim.[73] This news clip introduces the episode that deals with race in America and not only frames Ali's death in terms of his Muslim religion, but also frames the struggle for Black equality as historical and ongoing.

Episode 13: Women

Before Episode 13, "Women," the news clip reports on several local French government attempts to ban the burkini, only to have the French Supreme Court say that banning the modest style of bathing suit was unconstitutional.[74] Those who favored the ban suggested that wearing the burkini incited religious animosity.[75] The clip frames clothing as an important political, religious, and ideological marker. In the episode, there are different opinions presented about the hijab and issues of privacy and empowerment. Ana, representing a Latina, first-generation college student, states, "I've definitely read stuff about like how the hijab's empowering. Like you don't have to do your hair. You don't have to do your makeup. You can be yourself. Some people feel more like safe." Heather, a white millennial character, says, "The best way that I've heard it put is, it privatizes a woman's sexuality. A woman can be who she is and be successful without having to have her sexuality on display. By saying you need to take off your hijab, that's saying you need to be forward with your sexuality or you're oppressed." The news clip sets the agenda that we are talking about Muslim women, and frames clothing as a political issue.

Episode 16: Refugees and Immigrants

Finally, before Episode 16, "Refugees and Immigrants,"[76] the news clip is about the drowning of Syrian refugees in the Mediterranean and it includes an iconic picture of the limp body of a drowned boy. The use of the image helps frame the issue of refugees and immigrants as a humanitarian crisis. In the audio that accompanies the picture, we hear "An estimated 5,000+ people have drowned in the Mediterranean Sea in 2016 while seeking refuge from Syria's civil war," and we hear the presidential candidates' positions toward refugees. Hillary Clinton says, "We're facing the worst refugee crisis since the end of World War II and I think the United States has to do more." Donald Trump, on the other hand, tells a cheering crowd, "I'm putting the people on notice that are coming here from Syria as part of this mass migration, that if I win, if I win, they're going back." As an audience, we get to see not only that we should think about refugees and immigrants (agenda-setting), but how both candidates used the news to frame the refugee issue and prime their audiences. Clinton appears calm and rational and is suggesting that as a welcoming country, the United States should take in more refugees from Syria, while Trump appeals to his supporters' fear of "mass migration." Trump is priming the audience to think that a candidate should be judged by what the candidate will do to protect America from the wrong kind of immigrants and refugees. The episode that follows highlights disparate views toward Muslims in America that match the two frames presented in the news clip.

Ending the Play

In addition to the twelve news clips that introduced episodes, a thirteenth clip ended the play. The clip presented the news that Trump had won the electoral college vote while losing the popular vote. The last words of the play announced, "President-elect Trump vows to Make America Great Again." Here the news is setting the agenda for the audience to ponder the fact that Donald Trump won the election and, potentially, to have them think about what the election continues to mean for the country.

NEWS IN THE INTERVIEWS

Just as the playwrights used the news to set agendas, frame issues, and prime our audience, our interviewees, and thus the characters in the play, used news to make sense of their worlds. When they were interviewed, we asked people, "Does this discussion around Islam remind you of any other political conversation in history?" and "Can you remember how old you were when you first heard about Islam talked about in politics?" Throughout the play, audience members hear characters mention the importance of 9/11, the civil rights movement, and other events as touchstones of their lives.[77] The play reminds us that people use a variety of sources to make sense of their world. And, not surprisingly, people interpret the same event in dramatically different ways.

9/11

Multiple interviewees mentioned the attack on the United States on September 11, 2001 as a frame for understanding Islam. It was the most talked about news event in the play. We wanted to show the diversity of frames people used to interpret 9/11 and we used different episodes to do this. In Episode 3, "Millennials," Heather, who represents a white millennial character, talked about how the event impacted her generation:

> I think that people from our generation have been fed like this idea of Islam that's very, like it oppresses women and it's anti-liberal and it's anti-intellectual and it's violent, and so like that's been the way that the media and everything has talked about Islam since we were kids, cause we're in this, you know, post-9/11 world of consciousness.

Marco, who is presented as a Latino millennial, says:

> I vividly remember 9/11 . . .. It was the first time I saw my dad crying and that is traumatizing for
> any eight-year-old. I didn't understand what was going on, I didn't understand the significance of the
> building falling down. But I remember being quite disturbed because I could see how upset my parents
> were.

The play also includes how a Muslim and a Sikh character remember and frame 9/11 differently from the millennials. In Episode 4, "Learning for Yourself," Saleem, who represents a Muslim man, states:

> Starting like a few weeks after 9/11, there was a string of arson attacks on convenience stores, there were
> like nine in a row, like every other day there was one happening. All Muslim owned businesses in this
> city. (Pause) So my dad has a convenience store and I used to work there, when I was in high school.
> Those people have seen me grow up. I was a kid, I was nobody. So I got asked about jihad and about
> sharia law and stuff. Out of this seventeen, eighteen-year-old kid they would ask these questions. My
> dad he would just tell me to keep my mouth shut.

Hari, the character of a Sikh father, in Episode 6, "Sikhs," states, "I specifically remember after 9/11, my
dad would just say, 'Hey you can't go out. You shouldn't go out.'" By including different voices around 9/11, the
audience is given the opportunity to see that their framing of 9/11 is just one interpretation of the news event. It
is one of the play's attempts to open space for more diversity and complexity of thought around key news events
and ideas.

Civil Rights Movement and Black Lives Matter

Multiple interviewees used the civil rights movement to make sense of their experiences, often to different ends.
In Episode 12, "Erased," the civil rights movement and Black Lives Matter are mentioned by the character,
Donny, who represents a gay Republican interviewee:

> I'm Episcopalian which tends to lean left, and I tend to lean right. The Episcopal Church, to me, has the
> opposite thinking than I do. They're trying to be politically correct. They're actually condemning their
> own while excusing the bad behavior. The church was on the wrong side of the civil rights movement. I
> think they're on the wrong side of this because they're not thinking this through.

Donny is talking about the Episcopal Church's outreach to Muslims. He felt that his church didn't support the
civil rights movement. He thought this was wrong. Now that his church is supporting Muslim outreach, he again
thinks his church is wrong. He is presenting his argument within a historical context (i.e., civil rights movement
vs. Muslim outreach).

In another spot in the same episode, Donny continues, "Black Lives Matter, to me that's a very hateful group.
It's very racist, it's very hateful . . .. The whole Black Lives Matter movement is based on a lie." This last statement

is followed by Joshua, who is presented as a Black Muslim with a PhD and states, "The Black Lives Matter movement is a civil rights movement. The Black Lives Matter movement is the women's suffrage movement. The Black Lives Matter movement goes to freedom back in slavery days. This movement is not new." In this case, it is Joshua who is framing the current state of Blacks within a historical context, "I just think of everything that we have gone through in this country as Black people, yet we are still here: the Tuskegee experiment, lynchings, Jim Crow, and you do all this to try to wipe us out. And I learned that really, Islam was the foundation of where I got that."

Other Stories

Besides 9/11 and the civil rights and Black Lives Matter movements, other news events or issues were brought up by people to help frame their arguments and make their point. For example, in Episode 6, Hari tries to explain what Sikhs go through when they are mistaken for Muslims by citing the mass shooting that took place on August 5, 2012 in Wisconsin: "In Oak Creek, Wisconsin, where somebody went into a Sikh temple and started killing because he thought they were Muslims. That's really what happened. He shot nine or ten folks who died. Policemen died, and policemen were injured."

In the "Introduction," Myra, the character of a Jewish grandmother, relates the difference between focusing on terrorism and focusing on religious zealots. She uses the 1995 Timothy McVeigh bombing of the Alfred P. Murrah Federal Building to make her point. "I mean, we could be discussing terrorism, which is, you know, not only Muslims. I mean, who blew up the building in Oklahoma City? A good, red-blooded American."

In Episode 5, "Political Correctness," there is the issue of climate change that is used by Barry, who represents a white, conservative college professor, to show how the right and left both use political correctness as a tactic:

> I see political correctness as a tactic on both sides of the ideological spectrum. My experience is that it is a tactic of the left used to shut down debate by shaming people or just defining them as bad, racist, sexist, whatever. Now again, if you go into political conservative circles, whether it's a church or just a bunch of rednecks on a hunting trip, there'll be a different kind of political correctness there. God forbid you raise the idea of climate change, for example, you're a nutjob if you say that.

Again, people who were interviewed used news stories to help them make their points, frame their arguments, and present their insights.

CONCLUSION

Agenda-setting, framing, and priming are key constructs for those who study political communication and the news. *To Be Honest* uses different news clips to signal what audiences should be thinking about, to help frame issues, and to prime the audience to think in specific ways about political candidates and their policies. And, interestingly, those who were interviewed and whose words were included in the play often used news events to help tell their own personal stories. Whether it was 9/11, the civil rights movement, Black Lives Matter, or issues surrounding climate change, people used the news to help frame their arguments and prime the audience to think about politicians and issues in specific ways.

Finally, though not conceptualized within the news-social-psychology literature, the play itself sets an agenda for the audience to think about perceptions of Islam. The purpose of the play is to provide a variety of perceptions about Islam during the 2016 presidential campaign and to use the voices of the different characters to frame issues in ways that often contradict each other. By presenting the verbatim voices of Muslims, Sikhs, Christians, Jews, Republicans, Democrats, members of an anti-Muslim group, refugee advocates, grandmothers, millennials, and others, we framed the narrative to present a clash of unfamiliar and uncomfortable ideas that we hoped would lead to reflection and productive conversation.[78]

CHAPTER THREE

THE MUSLIM QUESTION IN THE 2016 PRESIDENTIAL ELECTION: REGULATING SPEECH, NATIONHOOD, AND GENDER

Habiba Noor

Donald J. Trump's announcement in 2015 proposing a total and complete shutdown of Muslims entering the United States set the stage for the research that became the script of *To Be Honest*. While there were multiple instances that could be used as a defining moment of the 2016 presidential election, this turned Muslim belonging in the United States into a campaign issue. The research that resulted in the script for the play began with the question: *A lot has been said about Islam in this election. What have you heard?* In this chapter, I demonstrate that responses to this question say less about Islam and more about what it means to be an American. The presidential election of 2016 marks a significant shift in the representation of Islam. Over two decades, stories about Muslims and Islam have shifted from foreign stories on terrorism to a domestic issue on Muslim belonging. The Muslim population in the U.S. is less than 1%, yet the narrative of political Islam loomed large over the political imagination.

This chapter analyzes how the diverse, intimate, and competing voices in *To Be Honest* engage the figure of the Muslim in ways that recast the contemporary American project as a question. The political scientist Anne Norton argues that the contemporary focus on Islam echoes the way in which Judaism was questioned in 19th century Europe. She writes that what Marx described as the "Jewish question" has been replaced by the "Muslim question." Like Judaism in years past, Islam has become a central axis around which Europeans have come to relate to their own liberal political principles of liberty, secularism, and national identity.[79] While the question of Muslim belonging has a deeper history in Europe, we saw that it took hold of the American political landscape during the 2016 election. *To Be Honest* highlights the way that Islam continues to be perceived as a domestic threat—not simply a threat to security but to the possibility of fundamental democratic rights, such as free speech, privacy, and equal protection under the law. Importantly, the play also signals how Muslim inclusion into the American story can simultaneously challenge *and* affirm the possibility of a genuinely multiethnic and multireligious society. While the Muslim question reveals a nearly irreconcilable divide among citizens, it also points to certain ambiguities about what constitutes the *soul* of America.

The idea that Muslim and Western civilization are fundamentally at odds is arguably a foundational idea for many in Europe and America. Samuel Huntington's *Clash of Civilizations* continues to be one of the most commonly read texts by college freshman in the U.S.[80] His argument reinforces the orientalist claim that conflicts have cultural roots and erases the impact of politics, specifically the social, economic, and institutional legacies of colonialism. Huntington has been widely criticized as promoting a racialized narrative of "us versus them."[81] It presupposes a distinction—if not incompatibility—between Western and Islamic societies and ignores the multiple ways that societies have historically influenced each other.[82] But the discourse around Islam during the election, which is exemplified in *To Be Honest*, reconfigures who is "us" and who is "them." The Trump presidency signals a shifting notion of the us and them divide within the American public. The fault lines of this divide center around competing commitments to principles of liberty, plurality, and religious freedom. It echoes what political scientist Peter O'Brien calls a "clash within civilizations."[83] *To Be Honest* gives voice to this clash. This chapter draws directly from the script to analyze the multiple ways that our respondents spoke to three polarizing issues: "political correctness," competing obligations to the nation, and gender.

The Emerging Muslim Question

Before analyzing the centrality of Islam in the 2016 election, it is essential to situate the way in which Islam figured into American politics historically. Islam became headline news immediately after the 9/11 attacks, and while this was the first time many Americans were confronted with the religion as a political force, it was by no means the first time Muslims became a feature in American news. Examples include stories of the Palestinian uprisings, the Iranian Revolution, and the Nation of Islam from the latter half of the 20th century. These stories of Islam have been linked with political resistance and violence.

If we go further back, we see that Muslims were generally written out of American history. In her work on Islam in early American history, historian Denise Spellberg writes that for the "founders," Islam was thought of as the hypothetical "other." Thomas Jefferson, through his readings of Locke, understood that religious freedom should be for all religions. This included a circumstance where a Catholic, a Pagan, or even a "Mahometan" (Muslim) may even be president. For Jefferson, the Muslim posed a theoretical test to the idea of secularism and religious freedom. He wrote, "neither pagan, nor Mahometan, nor Jew ought to be excluded from the commonwealth because of his religion."[84] In fact, this sentiment inspired the Virginia Statute for Religious Freedom in 1786.

But despite Jefferson's imaginings of hypothetical Muslim leaders, we cannot ignore the fact that Muslims arrived in America in the seventeenth century as enslaved Africans, who were denied the right to practice and pass on their religion. Scholars estimate that nearly a third of the enslaved Africans were members of Muslim tribes. Among them was Omar ibn Said, an Islamic scholar who was not only literate in Arabic but was also a scholar of Islamic law. This history is significant as it underscores the racial gap in the American historical narrative around the question of religious liberty.[85]

The presence of Muslims in America at the turn of the century was primarily understood through a racial logic. This was exemplified in a 1942 court case in which Yemeni Muslim Ahmad Hassan sought to prove he was white. At the time, immigration and naturalization were only permitted for "races indigenous to the Western hemisphere."[86] Hassan was denied citizenship because a judge determined he did not meet the criteria for whiteness. Aside from his "dark skin," his religion was a part of the "Mohammedan world and that a wide gulf separates their culture from that of the predominately Christian peoples of Europe."[87] Scholar Moustafa Bayoumi uses this example to argue that in 1942, religion determined race. But for white European Muslims—like ethnic Tatars from Belarus—religion was not relevant to their migration to Ellis Island. Members from this community started one of the oldest mosques in Brooklyn in 1907 without controversy.[88]

By the 20th century, the religion of Islam became a controversial part of the larger phenomenon of Black nationalism. In 1959, Islam was introduced to mainstream U.S. audiences via the television documentary *The Hate That Hate Produced*. This program framed Islam as a violent and radical insurgent movement espoused by Elijah Muhammad and the Nation of Islam that posed a significant threat to race relations in America.[89] After the 1965 Immigration Act barred race-based quotas, the Muslim population increased migration from Muslim countries in the Middle East and South Asia. The stories of the Iranian Revolution in 1979 and Palestinian resistance to Israel fueled the narrative of Muslims as "violent." The representation of Muslims in news[90] and entertainment[91] was driven by orientalist stereotypes. Muslims were not considered a part of the nation, as they were perceived as simultaneously foreign and unassimilated to the mainstream. As late as the 1990s, Islam was not perceived as a conventional American religion.

Representation of Islam and Muslims changed drastically after the 9/11 attacks, when Islam and Muslims were thrust into the spotlight. In the years that followed 9/11, Islam continued to be seen as a problem. Journalists sought to explain "why they hate us."[92] They solicited explainers on the religion of Islam to frame motivations of the terrorists. Terrorism was understood as a religious, not a political force. And a common refrain from those who sought to defend the religion was that "Islam had been highjacked." Interfaith and other civic organizations brought Muslims into public discussions as it was often suggested that in order to understand 9/11, Americans ought to learn about Islam and get to know their Muslim neighbors. Muslims of diverse backgrounds, who represented middle and upper middle-class professionals, emerged as a visible contingent of the U.S. population. The Pew Research Center conducted research on Muslim American identity and data began to show that Muslims are good neighbors, good citizens, and tolerant of diverse religious communities in the United States.[93] The prevailing narrative, which was echoed by political leaders on the left and right, was that despite Islamist violence, Islam was a "religion of peace" and that Muslim neighbors are loyal citizens. This became what anthropologist Mahmood Mamdani critically characterized as a story of "good Muslim, bad Muslim."[94] The good Muslim is moderate in politics and religion, while the bad Muslim is extremist, literalist, and vehemently critical of American foreign policy.

Despite this wider recognition of Muslims in the 2000s, this era stimulated the rise of an anti-Muslim movement networked through a series of organizations like the Center for Security Policy and ACT! For America.[95] These organizations and their leaders were featured in a flurry of national news reporting during the summer of 2010 related to the "Ground Zero Mosque" controversy. Activists like Pamela Geller, a conservative blogger, and Robert Spencer, founder and director of "Jihad Watch," organized protests in opposition of an Islamic center in downtown Manhattan located blocks from the World Trade Center.[96] Geller and Spencer referred to this center as a "Victory Mosque" to advance their claims that Muslims desire conquest in America.

A deeper look into their movement linked these activists as central nodes of a well-funded "Islamophobia Industry."[97] Part of the Islamophobia Industry's project was to formulate model legislation that sought to ban sharia law. The work of this network gained prominence through social media and right-wing media sources like Breitbart, Info Wars, and the Drudge Report; these media outlets propagated stories of a Muslim "fifth column" presence that sought to wage a "stealth jihad."

In the years immediately after the attacks in 2001, movement leaders like Spencer, Geller, and former Reagan advisor Frank Gaffney were considered fringe, but from 2009 to 2016, the ideas of the Islamophobia network[98] moved steadily toward the mainstream.[99] Evidence suggests that Trump relied on this network to inform his rhetoric on Islam and immigration policy. In December 2015, he referenced the Center for Security Policy (CSP), an organization that he described as "very highly respectable people, who I know, actually."[100] This right-wing think tank, founded by Frank Gaffney, is a key resource for the Islamophobia network and is described by the Southern Poverty Law Center as a "conspiracy-oriented mouthpiece for the growing anti-Muslim movement in the United States."[101] In a statement entitled "Preventing Muslim Immigration," the Trump campaign refer-enced a CSP study which stated "25% of those (Muslims) polled believed that violence against Americans is justified as a part of the global jihad and 51% agreed that Muslims in America should have the choice of being governed according to Sharia."[102] As researchers, our goal was to consider how these ideas manifest and circulate among audiences. The power of these organizations and the network more broadly is the way the anti-Muslim sentiment becomes legitimized through statistics that problematically frame the threat. In Episode 9, "Debating Islam," the character Jay says that he "heard of a fellow in the media that conducted a survey among Muslims in America. He asked: 'If you had your preference between the American way of legal system or the sharia law, which would you prefer?' Two to one it was sharia law." By including these claims about sharia in the script, our intention is not to magnify the Islamophobic anti-sharia discourse. This specific reference affirms the power of the Islamophobia industry in framing broader anti-Muslim sentiment in America.

Method of Analysis

My analysis in this chapter stems from theories of media and cultural studies with an emphasis on media audi-ences. I see the words of the characters as information that helps us understand how people make meaning of the political discourse, but their ideas are wholly unique or singular. Media and cultural studies understand meaning making as a *social* process, where meanings are derived from a set of available discourses.[103] In this current era of social media saturation these processes are magnified by the filter bubbles we inhabit and the increasing suspi-cion of news itself. While the 2016 election will be remembered for the stories of misinformation through outside influence on Facebook, Twitter, Info Wars, and other sources, this research does not track the accuracy of political knowledge and the impact of false stories. The goal of audience responses is not simply to understand the accuracy of representation, but in how representations translate into social relations and values. Specifically, how does the circulation of media discourse itself intervene on questions of belonging? And how can we analyze language as a site to understand the way such discourses circulate?[104] It follows that political constituencies become mobilized through discourse rather than the "reality" of events and policies themselves. More specifi-cally, the political discourse around Islam and migration has intervened on what it means to be an American. Much of the culture war that came out of the Trump campaign and ensued throughout his presidency has been fought through language. Below, I describe how debates on how to "name the enemy" spiraled into broader debates around political correctness.

Masking the Threat

In a town hall in September 2016, an audience member asked President Obama why he did not use the term "radical Islamic terrorist" when discussing acts of terror like the Orlando shooting. Obama acknowledged that organizations like Al Qaeda and ISIS "pervert and distort" Islam as an excuse for "barbarism" and that there is "no religious rationale" for their actions. He continued, "But what I have been careful about when I describe these issues is to make sure that we do not lump these murderers into the billion Muslims that exist around the world, including in this country, who are peaceful and who are responsible."[105] This response did not satisfy Senator Ted Cruz who, a few months earlier convened a hearing to investigate the use of language to describe terrorism. Cruz argued that on this issue, "political correctness" was getting in the way of national security.[106] The desire to use the phrase "radical Islamic terrorism" was an effort by leaders on the right to make the connection between violence and the religion of Islam. For Cruz, using that phrase is a first step in identifying the problem; it would serve to justify policies that target Muslim communities like immigration, surveillance, and increased policing. The irony here is that those policies were features of the Obama and Bush administrations.[107] Nevertheless, in contrast to the current administration,[108] both took care in their rhetoric to not publicly demonize American Muslims as the enemy. To be sure, both Obama and Cruz sought to manage public understanding of Islam; while the Obama and Bush administrations were careful not to name the religion as the problem, Cruz framed their policy as a deliberate attempt to erase the origin of the conflict. The contest over naming Islam as the source of terrorism circulated in popular discourse and emerged as a theme in the research. In Episode 5, "Political Correctness," we capture how this debate intervenes on social relations.

Jay, who unlike Patrick and Betty, read widely on Islam, said "We should be able to talk about the blemishes of Islam, (but) if we do that then we are labeled as Islamophobic." For Jay, the Islamic threat is not simply terrorism, but for him the religion itself undermines American liberty. Not only is this treatment of Islam a violation of free speech, but he also sees Islam as a broader threat to the Constitution. In "Debating Islam," Jay frames Islam not as a religion but as a "cause" and part of this cause is to "change the American legal system." The real reason to name Islam is not to appeal to Muslim sensitivities—in fact for Jay, Muslim sensitivities are a weapon used by domestic Islamists to wage a "stealth jihad."

Patrick, a former union member and Democrat, resents the regulation of language around Islam; he says, "There seems to be a more anti-Christian movement. It's okay to say negative things about Christianity in our society. It's not politically correct to say negative things about Islam in public." For Patrick, Obama's reluctance to call terrorism "Islamic" creates a double standard for Christianity. It reinforces his belief that Islam is unjustly rewarded a "special status." This idea of Islam being immune to public criticism was echoed by another character named Betty.

Betty, a middle-aged Christian, was interviewed along with other members of her Bible study. In response to our question on Islam in the elections she said, "What have I heard about Islam? Nothing, because there's like a deference towards Islam. We have heard about refugees, but not about Islam. *We don't really want to talk about it very much because we're afraid we're going to insult somebody.*" [emphasis added]. Although this specific response was not included in our script, it exemplifies the perceived nexus between refugees, security, and political correctness. She recognizes that naming the violence as Islamic has the potential to cause insult or injury to "somebody"—which arguably would be the Muslim community. Ironically, this view aligns with Obama's statement at the town hall. But unlike Obama, who believes that terrorism is a distortion of the religion, she thinks violence is fundamentally linked to Islam. Patrick expresses a broader view of this insult; he says, "You dare speak your mind about maybe we shouldn't have Islam, then everyone's going to say you're a racist. You're a bigot." Patrick is not closely allied with the Muslim community, therefore when he says that "everyone's going to say you're a racist," he likely means non-Muslims. In this regard, to name and criticize Islam is not seen as injurious to just Muslims but to non-Muslims as well.

While much of the research on Islamophobia directs attention toward the injury of this racism on Muslims, the responses of Ellen, Heather, and Marcos exemplify the impact of anti-Muslim statements on social relations for people who are not Muslim. The episode "Political Correctness" ends with Ellen, who says, "I'm learning about the prejudices of my close friends that were under the table until Donald Trump got the nomination. Just at the dinner table there are conversations that disturb me to no end with close, close friends. The way they echo some of Trump's comments about Muslims . . .. They have deep-seated prejudices that I wasn't aware of." Here we see an example of how Ellen's opinion of her friends changed after hearing about their "prejudices." While she does not describe the way in which these relationships changed, Marco and Ana share an experience from social media. Marco said: "I don't ever unfriend anybody on Facebook. But, an ex-girlfriend of mine from middle school posted something about Obama's Muslim agenda is the reason why that attack happened. I deleted her." Ana also described how a debate on a Facebook post comparing Trump to Hitler led her to "unfriend" someone. The significance of Ellen, Ana, and Marco's comments is that the offense caused from voicing Islamophobic sentiments is not limited to Muslims and reminds us that unregulated speech has powerful social consequences. These examples underscore the fact that the injury of Islamophobic speech, while directed at Muslims, was felt by people outside of the Muslim community and contributes to an increasingly divided constituency.

Competing Obligations to the Nation

In this section, I draw again from Jay and Ellen to analyze these competing obligations to the nation. I chose them again because compared to the rest of the characters, they would see themselves as activists to confront this changing demographic. Yet, their activism comes from vastly different places. An analysis of Ellen and Jay's views on migration and refugees underscores two fundamentally competing views of American nationalism. While both would see themselves as patriotic, they express competing obligations to the nation. The figure of the Muslim refugee forces the question of who is entitled to the American promise of liberty.

Drawing from Jay's interview, we see that he is not opposed to migration in principle, but he believes that "we have no moral obligation to let anybody who applies to come into this country . . . we should only allow people who are going to contribute, who are not a threat to the country, that already share some of the values that we share and that we as a country believe are valuable." So while he is not anti-immigration in principle, he believes the migrant should not have values that conflict with American democracy. In this regard, he sees pious Muslims as an existential threat to the core principles and ethics of the nation because of their desire to usurp American laws with sharia law. He said:

Foreign people leads to foreign law which undermines our country. All the number of refugees that we were having come into our country, should we allow all of them to just apply Zimbabwe or Somalia or whatever cultural norms they want to apply? . . . We've never done that in the history of our country before, to allow foreign laws.

Jay's allegation that foreign law is a threat to America reflects the broader "anti-sharia" movement which falsely characterizes a Muslim plan to impose Islamic law in American courts. The leaders of the anti-sharia legislation conjured horror stories of stoning, lashings, and beheadings in ISIS-controlled lands and in Afghanistan and Saudi Arabia. Lawyer David Yelrushalmi, a leader in the anti-sharia movement, exploited these fears to legislate against Islamic law in states throughout the U.S.[109] Legal scholar Asifa Quraishi Landes writes that the U.S. Constitution does not bar the use of religious law so long as it does not violate the Constitution. Islamic law urges Muslims who live in non-Muslim countries to follow the law of the land.[110] Like the Christian Canaan Law or Jewish Halaqa, sharia is the Islamic ethical moral code. This code, much like the Constitution, is open to multiple interpretations and rulings. And the greatest application of these codes is with regard to families, specifically rules of marriage and divorce. And if the specific divorce and marriage law (i.e., polygamy, child marriage, or female circumcision) does not comply with the U.S. Constitution, then the law is not permissible.

Ellen's response to the changes in political culture lie in sharp contrast to Jay. She draws on the soft nationalist ideals of American liberty and freedom in her volunteer work welcoming refugees from diverse backgrounds to the United States. In her interview, she describes the day-to-day challenges posed by the *lack* of resources offered by the state for refugee services. While children can receive Medicaid until they are 18, parents must learn to navigate the bureaucracy of the meager American welfare system to receive food stamps and will often work low wage jobs. The center where she volunteers resettled thousands of refugees since 2010, until the Trump presidency drastically cut the number of refugees allowed to enter the U.S. Ellen's words reflect pro-refugee, anti-Islamophobia views that have become central to the liberal, anti-Trump discourse. For Ellen, the plight of refugees creates an imperative for American citizens to help. In her interview she says: " . . . we as citizens have an obligation to help people get their feet on the ground and show them how hard work can pay off for them in the long run. The good news is that many people are going to college. They are graduating. The students make incredibly good students. Education is one of the best things about America."

For Ellen, opening borders to those in need becomes an *obligation* of this country. The success of refugees affirms her belief in the American promise of liberty and opportunity. Their stories affirm the value of hard work and animate the liberal vision of American exceptionalism afforded by freedom of speech, religious liberty, and equal rights for women. In America, she witnesses the necessity of Iraqi refugees putting aside sectarian differences to achieve the dream together. But Ellen understood this dream will not be realized immediately. Ellen exemplifies the "soft nationalism" of the liberal American who uses the plight of the refugee to affirm liberal ideals. But liberal ideals and the nation are under threat by the nativist impulses reflected in the Trump agenda, which challenges the universality of the American dream, and excludes people on the basis of religion. For Ellen, refugees also underscore the fact that the current economic climate of low wages and poor healthcare undermines the possibility for freedom. Liberty becomes threatened by the lack of social welfare. She has seen a few refugees return to their home countries because of the demanding expectations of workers with low paying jobs. The crucial threat to the American dream is not open borders, but the looming economic inequality and the treatment of the working poor. Opposing Trump's immigration policy becomes the imperative; because for Ellen, the obligation to the nation includes maintaining the possibility of the American dream for migrants around the world.

Gender and the "Clash of Civilizations"

A recurring theme that emerged through our discussions of Islam was gender. Our research did not include a specific question on gender in Islam, but despite this, many participants addressed the issue of women's rights in Muslim societies. What I argue here is that discussions about the role of gender in Islam wage claims on the basis of a "clash of civilizations" narrative. The way women's rights are spoken of in *To Be Honest* brings the imagination of civilizational conflict to a level that is intimate; for some, like Pastor Bill, Islamic "views" are fundamentally anti-woman: "That's the teaching of Muhammad. He puts women lower than he puts the Jews." But for others like Ellen, the wearing of hijab can be read as "a feminist act." Rather than framing women's clothing as fundamentally antimodern and backward, she assimilates it into the battle against patriarchy and does not negate its possible inclusion in the West.

Here, I analyze how Heather, Ellen, Karen, and Pastor Bill's views present Muslim women in relation to the idea of the "Clash of Civilizations," but before doing so, it is useful to revisit how the narrative of the "oppressed Muslim woman" was constructed through the colonial encounter. In *Women and Gender in Islam*, historian Leilah Ahmed describes how this trope was used to justify the colonial project. Lord Cromer, the British Consul General of Egypt in the late 1800s, famously believed that women's oppression is symbolized by the veil or hijab. Cromer, along with Egyptian modernizers, linked Western clothing with modernization. In this regard, civilizational advancement was linked to Westernization. Ahmed highlights Cromer's double standard on women's rights; while he uses "women's oppression" to justify intervention in Egypt, back in England he famously did not support women's suffrage.[111]

Over 100 years later, the story of women's rights was central in justifying militarization in the U.S. In 2001, George and Laura Bush centralized the oppression of women as a rationale for war in Afghanistan and used this issue to mobilize the Feminist Majority Foundation to support military intervention.[112] The blue "shuttlecock burqa" became the shorthand symbol for women's oppression in Afghanistan. But while gender injustice continues to be a problem in Egypt and Afghanistan, both Cromer and the war in Afghanistan focused the injustice on clothing as opposed to factors like poverty, gender-based violence, and the lack of education.

In the early 2000s, analysis of Muslim women's dress moved from the colonial imperatives toward Muslim women in Europe and North America. While U.S. laws cannot legislate on the hijab because of the First Amendment, Muslim women's dress continues to be a policy issue in Europe and more recently Canada. There, the question has become, can Muslim women who adhere to religious dress codes assimilate into Western norms? Will the principles of secularism guarantee the freedom to practice their religion as they choose? During the summer of 2016, we heard stories from France reporting on the criminalization of the burkini. And while that ban was lifted later that year, the hijab continues to be banned in public schools. These bans are premised on a French secularism, or *laïcité*, which mandates freedom *from* religious interference in public life. This principle presumes that religious regulations impede freedom of thought. Muslim assimilation into France, therefore, can only be achieved by appropriating Western norms, which is why, arguably, integration continues to pose a challenge to French society, and in this regard, the civilizational clash has come home.

But while religious freedom in the United States guarantees the right to practice religion freely and gives women the right to wear hijabs, the hijab has a racializing force that frames Muslim women as the "other" and symbolizes their inability to assimilate into the U.S.[113] This barrier to integration can be used to support their exclusion. Returning to the script, Pastor Bill values diversity and does not seek to turn back the clock to his racist childhood in East Texas. He says, "I don't care who comes in, but they got to do it right. If they don't assimilate, they don't do well."

Unlike the more liberal women in her focus group, Karen "has a totally different view of Muslims." She draws her conclusions based on her years living in Pakistan where she had interactions with Afghan refugees. For Karen, the conflict *is* civilizational and her experience abroad is what gives her authority. The lower status of Afghan women was not necessarily their *fault* but rather an outcome of a flawed culture; in fact, she says "their culture sucks." Karen expressed concern about Islam's oppression of women and did not want to be perceived as a "crazed Trump person," but unlike Ellen, is skeptical that Islam can actually be a liberating force.

Heather, a college student, seeks to understand what the hijab affords, rather than what it takes away. Her view is that covering one's hair can be perceived as "empowering" and that it allows women to "be themselves." What Heather suggests is that the logic of the hijab lies in contrast with the contemporary logic of beauty in the West. Rather than serving as a tool for oppression, she perceives the hijab as a tool of "freedom." Heather echoes a specific understanding of the hijab that is common among Muslims themselves, who advocate for the hijab as a feminist act. But Heather's framework feeds into a dichotomy which frames the hijab as being in direct contrast to the beauty industry. Recent trends in social media have given space to Muslim women who don't see a conflict between religious obligations with the overall beauty industry. But Heather's discussion of women is significant because it leads her to challenge liberation of women in the West. She subverts the narrative of Muslim women's oppression when she says "what we don't see is how oppressed women in the West are . . . we're forced to obsess about our bodies. That can be deadly."

Karen and Pastor Bill frame Islam as fundamentally foreign and outside Western norms and as posing a threat to the American way of life. But Heather and Ellen view the American way of life as flexible. Rather than expecting Muslim women to conform to Western notions of beauty, fashion, and freedom, they draw on the Muslim perspective to reflect on their own practices and culture. In this regard, they believe in the fluidity of Western civilization itself.

The fluidity of civilization is embodied through Khadijah and Saleem. This is exemplified when Saleem says, "I never saw it (hijab) as a defining feature of a woman's faith." Khadijah, who wears a hijab and lives in the U.S., does not frame her religion in opposition to dominant society and does not live in the binary logic of East versus West. But despite this, she is often perceived as an outsider. We hear this in Episode 13, "Women," when she says: "We're not treated as normal citizens. Some companies put us in their ads here and there or have pictures of us at the mall or something, like [in] a hijab or whatever. We're still not normalized as any other citizen that just wears a headscarf. We are just not there yet."

Conclusion

In 2015, Trump's Muslim ban proposal compromised religious liberty and challenged race-based migration policies, which have been in place since the 1965 Naturalization Act. For his supporters, regulation of migration was justified because of the exceptional threat that Muslims posed. But for his opponents, the proposal signaled a violation of an American ideal. So how does the ban fit into the slogan of "making America great again"? For Trump and his supporters, they wished to shift the demographics to an era in which the Muslim presence did not evoke a question; a time when Muslims were not an American problem. For them, the conflict with Muslims is about civilization itself and thus, according to Jay, there should be no "obligation" to open borders to refugees or Muslims.

For liberal respondents like Ellen, Myra, Hari, and Sarita, Trump and his Muslim ban proposal activate a commitment toward the American principle of religious freedom and the idea of America as a site of refuge. Religious freedom in the United States serves as a rationale for America's greatness. Catholics, Jews, Sikhs, and Muslims have experienced marginality, but the religious freedom afforded by this country roots them into the broader American story. Trump's speech in December 2015 provoked competing obligations across the religious and political divide.

It is important to consider that Trump's rhetoric has become both normalized and resisted. On July 26, 2018, the Muslim ban, now known as the "travel ban," was upheld by the Supreme Court in a 5–4 decision. But on January 20, 2021, President Biden signed the executive order to reverse the Muslim travel ban on his first day of office. We should remember that during the 2016 Republican primary, Senator Lindsey Graham vehemently opposed Trump's initial proposal for the Muslim ban. Two years later, he praised Trump on Fox News after a truck attack in NYC for understanding "we are in a religious war."[114] This shift in views is a testament to the erosion of traditional Republican conservatism.

During a presidential debate with Donald Trump in 2020, Joe Biden famously used "*inshallah*," a commonly used Arabic term meaning "God willing." We can suspect that Biden's comfortable use of inshallah did not lead his critics to accuse him of being a secret Muslim, unlike the persistent belief among Republicans that Obama was concealing his religion. In fact, some have suggested that Biden's use of the term was a deliberate strategy to increase his popularity among Muslim voters. In her discussion of the Jewish question, Norton says that as "Jews became more American, Americans became more Jewish." She describes this as "reciprocal assimilation," where the assimilation does not have a singular direction of migrant to host society but is diffused. Despite the fact that the Muslim ban has become intrenched in legislation, Biden's language—along with an increased representation of Muslims in popular media—signals a horizon of "reciprocal assimilation" for Muslims in America. But this type of assimilation is not universally celebrated. The polarization that *To Be Honest* captures was arguably the early stages of the increasingly divided American populace. And despite efforts for national healing by listening to all sides, we must understand that the differences stem from deeply competing notions of what it means to be American.

CHAPTER FOUR

CONSERVATIVE EVANGELICAL INTERPRETATIONS OF ISLAM

Van Wagner

"Islam," not "Muslims," our conservative evangelical interviewees told us repeatedly. The majority of our twenty-four conservative evangelical interviewees, seventeen of whom spoke to us in focus groups, were at pains to emphasize that they took issue with Islam but did not harbor negative feelings toward Muslims. This was a crucial distinction for them. They did not wish to portray Muslims as evil or negative, merely incorrect and misguided, led astray by a falsehood. Muslims were not bad in and of themselves and as such could be brought to know the truth, to see light and reason, to become Christians. But Islam in its fundamental state was false and violent, opposed to everything they, their faith, and their democracy represent. In pinning their discomfort on the religion instead of its adherents, conservative evangelical interviewees and the characters who represent them in *To Be Honest* demonstrate the belief that Islam is and must be one single, negative way. Conservative evangelical Christians employ a strict reading of how Islam is and should be, in the same way that they read Christianity, the Bible, and their nation.

This chapter focuses on the importance of strict readings and absolutes in a conservative, American, evangelical worldview in which Islam plays the foil to all things Christian, American, and true. Here I explore interviewees' claims of truth and falsehood, the implications of religious exclusivism, and the use of singular literalist readings to understand both Christianity and Islam. This chapter does not attempt to define or circumscribe evangelicalism; the viewpoints of our conservative evangelical interviewees cannot be construed as necessary or normative for all evangelical groups. Two of our twenty-four conservative evangelical interviewees had differing views of Islam from their peers, which they attributed to years spent abroad in Muslim majority countries. I do not reference them in this chapter because they represent a different subset of conservative evangelical thought. This chapter illumines a perspective that features absolute truth claims and literalist readings of scripture. As I will show, binary morality extends beyond personal religious beliefs for the groups of evangelicals we interviewed. It shapes their worldview regarding civic and religious society more broadly.

I begin by setting out interviewees' claims of truth and falsehood about Christianity and Islam, before explaining how these claims are tied to their literalist readings of religion, culture, and governance. As I describe, the conservative evangelical Americans we interviewed exist in a moral world of *should*, where there are right and wrong ways to live in and think about the world. They believe in absolute truths and that the world's institutions are built around unalterable core substances. Accordingly, Islam is and can only be one way, just as with Christianity and the United States. The chapter concludes by suggesting how this worldview contributed to conservative religious groups' support for a president seemingly antithetical to their beliefs.

The "Only One Truth"

In Episode 10 of *To Be Honest,* Betty tells the audience, "I totally have issues with the religion of Islam because I just don't think it's the truth." This quote comes from a particularly fruitful focus group with members of an adult Sunday school. Betty's statement encapsulates much of what her cohort told us. The member of the focus group from whom Betty's statement was drawn continued to say:

> But with Muslims I think reach out to them, treat them fairly so on and so forth, but for a totally different reason: proselytizing. I want Muslims to know what I feel is the truth, and it has hope and peace because whatever you believe, if you don't have hope and you don't have peace, then you've got nothing. When you're alone at night in the dark, do you have hope and peace? Most of the Muslims . . . all of the Muslims actually that I've spoken with don't have hope and peace.

Here, Betty tells the interviewer that Islam is not the truth, unlike the faith the group wants to share by way of proselytism. What is more, this focus group member believes the church's truth will bring hope and peace, which cannot be attained through Islam. Angela, another interviewee in this group, expands upon this singular notion of truth:

> I know my truth, and I believe the truth. There can only be one truth . . . but because of what I believe, I'm going to treat [Muslims] with mercy and compassion because I want them ultimately to know the truth. When I am being friendly with those [Muslim] neighbors that we have, ultimately I want them to know the truth, so it is with a goal.

Angela sees the potential for her neighbors to believe in the truth, regardless of her neighbors' current beliefs. The group then discusses the importance of proselytism to Muslims. They agree that people should have access to the saving truth, and that the truth must win out over falsehood. There is one way to salvation in this vision, so sharing the gospel is the right and compassionate thing to do. Angela's Muslim neighbors have the opportunity to be on the side of truth. They currently believe a falsehood, an inherently risky one as members of the group point out. Alignment with religious falsehood is dangerous; only the Christian truth is right and salvific. These group members testify to the dualistic morality of their worldview, to the oppositional existence of true and false, right and wrong. There is no possible gradient of religious truth, at least between Christianity and Islam.

This type of thinking has been termed "religious exclusivism," a type of religious subjectivity that rejects the potential for a diversity of religious beliefs to have equal standing, in favor of a single, divine truth. But the people in our interview study differ from this broader category of "exclusivists" in important respects. Research on religious exclusivists has shown that exclusivism does not preclude nuanced beliefs about other religions.

Exclusivist Christians wrestle with their understandings of non-Christians' damnation, refusing to claim to know who is saved, themselves included.[115] There may be only one truth, they believe, but they refuse to claim certainty over judgments that ultimately lie in the hands of God. The members of the focus groups we interviewed however, express no such reservations. One told us: "I already know I'm going to heaven," and another added, "I don't fear so much for myself because I know where I'm going."

Our interviewees were convinced of the absolute truth of their beliefs over and against those of others. It is unclear how normative our interviewees' views are for conservative evangelicalism considering the diversity of the demographic. Perhaps we see denominational, cultural, or church-based differences reflected here. It is also possible that cultural change over time has impacted this stance with regard to Islam, considering the fact that anti-Muslim sentiment in the United States has only grown since the turn of the millennium.[116] Whatever the case, the danger of disbelief—particularly to Muslims as nonbelievers—is not a topic that goes unconsidered in conservative evangelical circles.

Islam as Monolithic

Having established the singularity of their vision and their desire for Muslims to share in it, our interviewees expounded on their concerns about Islam. These concerns extended outward, moving away from internal concerns about salvation of souls and into the nation and the world. Interviewees used civic rhetoric to justify suspicion on the basis of religion by describing Islam as anti-American, thereby turning Islamophobic stances into matters of national security.[117] In Episode 9 of the play, the character Jay illustrates this when he says: "They're here to take over the country, the radical Islamists. Their hope and dream is that the Islamic flag will be flying over the White House instead of the flag of the United States of America." In Jay's framework, the spiritual concern for Muslims shifts to a sociopolitical fear of Islam. In our focus groups, many respondents agreed that the United States government and legal system exist in opposition to Islam.

Jay stands out in the intensity of his belief that Islam has designs on the United States and its government. As a military man, his concern is national security. Jay details how "radical Islamists" would go about taking over the country. They would use violence, but also more subtle means of attack. Jay tells us that Muslims make use of subversive and manipulative techniques to harm the country from within. In Episode 16, Jay offers his interpretation of the concept of *taqiya*, saying "There's a principle of Islam that says, 'It's okay to even deny your faith if it's going to further the cause of Islam.' That's a little frightening." Though the intent of *taqiya* is to protect individuals who are under threat for their faith, Jay interprets it as part of a manipulative strategy used by Muslims to pass as non-Muslims and further the agenda of Islam in secret.

These ideas imply that radical Islamists will engage with U.S. law and government in order to subvert them. The mechanism here is sharia law. Several interviewees believe that sharia law is gaining a foothold in the United States via the implementation of sharia courts by Muslims in the government. Members of a men's Bible study group had much to say about this aspect of Islam. They spoke of Islam as a political entity and emphasized how the religion's goal is to impose sharia law on the world. These interviewees cited attempts to install sharia courts in the United States as evidence of Islam's mission to take over. They believe these courts are intended to subvert and replace U.S. law for both Muslims and non-Muslims. In reality, sharia courts in the United States do exist, but they act as resources for resolving family issues for those who request them.[118]

Alexander, a member of the men's study group, sees the threat of such courts already operating in multiple countries. He tells the group "right now there is eleven sharia courts, thirteen sharia courts that have been established in Britain. We see the same thing in France." He adds, "That is not assimilation." In this view, the establishment of sharia courts signals a lack of Muslim assimilation, and even opposition to the "Western" way of living. Alexander describes Muslims as actively choosing loyalty to a lifestyle that is at odds with the prevailing cultures and legal systems of their countries. There is a right way to be a Muslim and there is a right way to be an American or a European, he implies, and those two ways are not compatible. This means that there is an inherent conflict of interest when Muslims live as American and European citizens.[119]

Bethany, a member of a women's Bible study group belonging to the same church, talks about how Muslims "want a section" of her hometown "to practice sharia law." This is not only a local threat, she says. She agrees with Alexander that Muslims want sharia law to "take precedence" over United States law and describes how "they're trying to get that passed in several places." Bethany believes such a threat can exist because "we have Muslims in our government now, in our government in Washington D.C., and there have been many appointed to very high positions in the government." She believes that loyalty to a democratic government and loyalty to Islam are incompatible, and that Muslims might accrue power through intrigue and political involvement. All of these concerns about sharia law display the belief that Islam is not only a religion, but an ambitious political and legal entity.

Connor, another member of the men's group, makes a slightly different contribution. He says, "We had a municipal court judge in New York who took an oath on the Qur'an and not the Bible." This is the entirety of his statement, but the implications are weighty. Connor suggests that the Qur'an is incongruous with U.S. law and democracy, while Christianity and the Bible are not. Though Connor is not explicit about why exactly a judge taking an oath of office upon the Qur'an is an issue, a few possibilities stand out. One potential reason for Connor's belief is that U.S. law and culture are built on "Judeo-Christian values" and the Qur'an does not fit into that legal and cultural standard. A second possibility is that Connor believes the Qur'an does not promote some core elements of a democratic government, such as truth or liberty. Yet a third possibility for Connor's alarm is the belief that taking such an oath indicates allegiance to Islam and Sharia law over allegiance to the nation and U.S. law. In any of these cases, the United States and Christianity are allied on the same side of a binary. Connor implies that loyalty to Christianity is cooperative with loyalty to the nation, while loyalty to Islam is contradictory to loyalty to the nation. Islam becomes a totality on one side of a struggle in perceived opposition to Christianity and the United States on the other side.

Jay's thinking develops one aspect of this conflict. His view of Islam as a totality does not require him to align the United States government with Judeo-Christian principles. Jay says, "Islam is all wrapped up into one, so their loyalty, when they say, 'I'm loyal to Islam,' they are saying, 'I'm loyal to a political, economic, social, religious system called Islam.'" The crux of the conflict Jay sees is not only between Christianity and Islam, but also the United States and Islam. His understanding of Islam is that it is an all-encompassing system, broader than Christianity as a religion or the United States as a nation. Jay's belief that Islam is a "political, economic, social, religious system" is informed by a number of sources, including personal experiences during his military service, but also books he has read, and his involvement with an anti-Islam activist group.

In Episode 4, Jay says, "I read a book by Daniel Pipes over in the Desert Storm in '91 . . . It talked about the coming tide of Islam here in the United States."[120] It is possible that Jay's reading list also includes books like Mark Hitchcock's *The Coming Islamic Invasion of Israel*, and Grant Jeffrey's *War on Terror: Unfolding Biblical Prophecy*, publications by evangelical writers leveling sociopolitical criticisms at Islam through a Christian prophetic lens.[121] Books like these, along with anti-Islam statements by evangelical leaders like Pat Robertson and Jerry Falwell, impact the beliefs of the people who consume them. Our interviewees are not alone in this. Interviews with other consumers of conservative Christian media demonstrate the same patterns of religio-political ideas about Islam. For example, Amit Bhatia's respondents also expressed beliefs that Islam does not support democracy and that sharia law would be a danger to the American legal system.[122] As Jay tells us, these beliefs have existed since long before the 2016 election cycle or even the 9/11 attacks. They have merely gained traction in the intervening time. In 2011, the majority of conservatives believed that Islamic values and American values were at odds, and a majority of Fox News viewers believed that Muslims were attempting to establish sharia law in the U.S.[123] Our respondents and the media they consume were already engaged in discussion about the enmity between the U.S. and Islam before the 2016 presidential campaign began. For years, they had been framing anti-Islamic sentiment as concern for the nation. Civic framing justifies suspicion of a potentially dangerous Muslim "other" as a patriotic defense of the country and its ideals.

Jay continues in his interview to compare Islam to Christianity and the U.S. government in a way that reveals a core component of this patriotic defense belief. He says, "There is no Christian government in the United States. There is no Christian Constitution, it's the U.S. Constitution. They don't identify as a nation-state standpoint like Muslims do." He describes Christianity and U.S. democracy as compatible in separation: the U.S. government allows and defends religious freedoms, and Christianity abides by national laws and extends basic tolerance to other faiths. His beliefs depict Christianity as the poster child for First Amendment rights because it maintains a symbiotic but separate relationship with the government. According to Jay, Islam's politics and religion are inextricably intertwined and thus push the limits of what the First amendment can allow. Because of this perceived conflict, Jay—and interviewees who agree with him—are considering the paradox of tolerance,[124] albeit from a different direction than their liberal and non-Christian counterparts. They ask themselves if America, a nation whose first constitutional amendment guarantees religious freedoms, can be tolerant of a religion that they believe to be intolerant of other religions and political systems. The presence of "peaceful Muslims" serves as a kind of proof of the concept for liberal democracy and Christian tolerance, but to Jay, Islam pushes the limits of his country's democratic experiment and his religion's ability to coexist with others.[125] Jay, a Christian, a veteran, and an activist, feels called to defend his tolerant nation from what he perceives to be the threat of intolerance.

"The Perfect Muslim"

Our interviewees go on to judge Muslims according to the same interpretive framework they use to understand their own religion. The strict and literal approach to the Bible and Christianity that is often a hallmark of conservative Christian communities in the United States is transposed. In Episode 9 of the play, Jay essentializes Muslims who, in his view "pick and choose" what aspects of Islam they favor. "That's great," he says, "Sign me up. Give me a couple of million Muslims like that." He believes that Muslims can eschew aspects of their religion to live in peace with Christianity and democracy. But he goes on to argue that they are not acting like *true* Muslims. "A Muslim doesn't get to define what Islam is," Jay says. "Muhammad does. Because it says [in the Qur'an], 'Muhammad is the perfect Muslim.'" Jay insists that these Muslims' personal experiences of their religion are not valid forms of Islam. There is one way to be a Muslim, according to Jay, and that is for individuals to adhere to his idea of a literalist interpretation of Islam.

Muslims the world over interpret their religion in myriad ways. Culture, history, gender, social status—all these and more play roles in what religious adherents value most from their traditions. With over a billion Muslims worldwide, Islam is diverse in ways that Jay does not acknowledge. Instead, Jay asserts that Muslims who are peaceful are actually not "good Muslims" because they do not accurately represent "true" Islam. About peaceful Muslims, he says, "you're a good Muslim from my perspective, but you're not a good Muslim from Muhammad's perspective."

Muhammad is one of the most important figures in the religion of Islam. He is the religion's founder, and thought to be a prophet, according to most of Islam's many branches. Perceived disrespect toward Muhammad has had violent consequences, as in the infamous case of the *Charlie Hebdo* cartoons. Yet Jay repeatedly brings up his own reading of Muhammad's significance within Islam. Jay says living like Muhammad means "marry someone who's six, chop people's heads off, lead twenty-six battles alone, order forty-seven other battles to go out and fight and kill others, order the assassination of women and men because they mocked him." Jay does not accept other potential lessons Muhammad leaves his followers, but essentializes him as a violent misogynist. Refusing to acknowledge that this is his own interpretation of a famously complex historical figure, Jay insists he is accomplishing a literal reading of the Qur'an. Diversity and disagreement exist even among Muslims who engage in conservative and literalist interpretations of Islam. But according to Jay, diverse interpretations do not impact the core truth of Islam because there is only one correct Qur'anic interpretation.

Jay understands that such diverse interpretations of religious texts exist, but he insists that deviation from his method of literalist reading is invalid. To make such arguments though, Jay must make use of interpretive tools. He discusses a shooting at a Planned Parenthood clinic in Colorado that was purported to serve Christian ideals. He argues that just because the shooter *said* he was a Christian, does not mean that he "is one." As Jay explains: "You can't find anything in the Christian doctrine that would support what [the Planned Parenthood shooter] said and did . . . the violence you see in the Old Testament was abrogated with Jesus Christ . . . You had to accept this, so it became much more peaceful." Here Jay performs an interpretive act, arguing that one aspect of a book must be understood by referring to another, later part. He performs the same interpretive act in reading the Qur'an, saying "when you hear a Muslim speak about the peaceful side of Islam, they are speaking about the Meccan phase. Sadly though, all those verses have been abrogated by violent verses in the last third of the Qur'an." Abrogation is a subject of much debate in Qur'anic exegesis. The Qur'an acknowledges abrogation but does not identify every instance of abrogation within itself. The process of identification falls to Muslim scholars who inevitably disagree. Any attempt to understand abrogation within the Qur'an requires interpretation of the reader. Jay's example demonstrates that while scriptural literalism may claim objectivity for the sake of authority, it cannot escape interpretive distance from the texts with which it engages.

William, another interviewee from the men's Bible study group, also shares opinions on who is and is not a proper Muslim when he describes interacting with a media campaign that emphasizes how Islam is widespread and diverse. Like Jay, William acknowledges that diversity among Muslims exists, but then asserts that many of these people are not "real Muslims":

I came across a video, and it's called "Meet a Muslim," and so it had all these Muslims. "Hi. My name is so-and-so, and I'm a pediatrician, and I'm married, and I have two girls . . . Hi. I'm Muslim, and I'm married to my life partner who is a man, and I drink wine . . . I look at that, and I'm going, "Those are cultural Muslims. Okay. They're not practicing Muslims." Because if they believed what the Qur'an says, they wouldn't be doing those things. If they did all those things in Saudi, they're dead. They will get their heads chopped off.

Here William makes the distinction between cultural and practicing Muslims. He believes that practicing Islam according to one particular reading of the Qur'an is the only correct way to practice Islam. William assumes that there are right and wrong ways to be a Muslim, and that the Qur'an can easily be shown to prescribe a clear and singular way of life to believers. This is where William's ignorance of Muslim experiences makes itself known. He did not speak about different Islamic schools of thought, sects, or theological debates. For example, whether an individual was a Shia or Sunni Muslim would probably mean little to William regarding their perceived status as a cultural or practicing Muslim. Such a distinction is not important for William or Jay as outsiders determining who the "real Muslims" are, though it is an important distinction for Muslims themselves. What is important for William and his group is how well they perceive Muslims to be adhering to Islam as they understand it.

William makes this metric more explicit as he discusses with his group the three types of Muslims: cultural/nominal, practicing/devout, and radical. They use the terms "cultural" and "nominal" to describe those Muslims who claim religiosity but do not engage much with their faith. The "practicing" and "devout" are a second type that they see as perhaps more comparable to themselves, actively engaged with their faith's orthodox rules, requirements, and traditions. The third type—those who are "radically" religious—are violent, former practicing/devout Muslims who have become radicalized. At this point in the discussion, it becomes unclear which of these types the men's group believes to be true Islam, the type that follows "what the Qur'an says." Alexander draws an analogy between radicalized Muslims and the Ku Klux Klan, who he says are not in any way Christian or Christ-like. This would seem to imply that radicalized Muslims do not represent Islam, but the topic shifts after he speaks.

William, on the other hand, seems to think that radical Muslims are more in line with Islam than not, lumping them together with practicing/devout Muslims when mentioning Muslim aversion to cultural mixing and interfaith marriage. He tells us that "your more devout and your radicalized Muslims have big problems. That's when you get into the honor killings and the disowning and cutting them off from the family." Further, he states that when radicalized Muslims commit violence, it is the cultural/nominal Muslims who speak out against them, saying that "they're crazy, that they're from the devil. That's from Hell. That's not for us. They're not Muslim." Ironically, William does not think that these cultural/nominal Muslims are "real" Muslims, and he disagrees with their assessment that radicalized Muslims are not Muslims. He does not allow insufficiently pious members of the faith authority on the topic of who is and is not Muslim, but he does allow himself, a Christian, that authority.

Some may look at this group's discussion of the types of Muslims and see hypocrisy, but these interviewees hold Muslims to a similar standard to the one in which they hold themselves in regard to piety. They expect a certain level of engagement from persons of faith for them to be considered members of the religions they claim. Alexander tells us, "You see that even across every religious spectrum. You have those that are more devout. You have those that are less devout, and in America, you see a predomination [sic] of people say they grew up in a Christian home. That doesn't necessarily make them Christian. Because they celebrate Christmas doesn't make them necessarily Christian." This men's group sees themselves as devout, pious people, a kind of Christian equivalent to the devout/practicing Muslims William described. The difference for them seems to be that they do not believe themselves to be in danger of violent radicalization, while they do believe devout/practicing Muslims are in such danger. This is because they see Christianity as inherently peaceful and Islam as inherently dangerous, so a movement toward a more perfect accord with "true" Christianity is a positive movement, while the same movement toward "true" Islam is a dangerous one.

Conclusion

Our interviews with evangelical Christians demonstrate how their preoccupation with absolute truth enables their strict readings of Islam, Christianity, and the United States. They present Islam as homogenous and all-encompassing, a monolith standing in opposition to Christianity and the democratic system of governance that has allowed it to flourish. To them, Islam is a complete social, political, religious system with one true manifestation: conquest by any means necessary. Because of the perceived totality of Islam, this group of interviewees understand Islam as a much greater threat to their nation and well-being than any other compet-ing faith. They see the goal of Islam as not only conversion, but also cultural and political dominance. They arrive at this conclusion because they believe that one particular interpretation of Islam—namely theirs—is the single correct interpretation. Though over a billion Muslims live varied lives around the globe, their actions and beliefs do not impact the core substance of Islam in these interviewees' eyes.

Taking all these ideas together can help us understand one way in which conservative American evangelicals engage with their country's current political climate. I have already discussed the way strict literalist readings of both the Bible and the Qur'an are part of a common evangelical interpretive framework, but this framework also applies to non-scriptural texts. As an example, consider originalist readings of the Constitution, which attempt to interpret the text in line with authorial intent or original meaning. But when conservative evangelicals who believe like our interviewees apply this interpretive framework, they take it beyond interpretations of written and spoken word. As we have seen, they apply it not just to scripture, but to Christianity and Islam as wholes. They believe there is one true way to both religions, and that cannot be changed by adherents. The same is true for national law as well as national culture. Just as there is a right way to be a Christian and a right way to be a Muslim, there is a right way to be an American.

The belief in a right way to be an American does not necessarily imply a defined and detailed set of traits that one must have. These interviewees speak in favor of First Amendment rights and freedom of expression, affirm-ing American diversity. In fact, the right way to be American that multiple interviewees emphasize—including liberals and non-Christians—means having no conflicts of interest with U.S. law and defending, even embrac-ing, the freedoms of others even if one fundamentally disagrees with conflicting beliefs. Interviewees brought up on more than one occasion the famous Evelyn Beatrice Hall quote, "I disapprove of what you say, but I will defend to the death your right to say it." On the surface, this stance is appealing and reasonable. But these inter-viewees also believe that Islam in particular is in conflict with U.S. law, and by extension with their own personal freedoms. Because of this conflict, the "practicing/devout" and "radicalized" Muslims discussed by members of William's Bible study cannot be true Americans by this metric.

This exclusive definition of Americanness is not a new problem. In years past, and often still today, Jews and Catholics have been harmed by the same kind of prejudices. Jews have been framed as eternal foreigners who are inherently loyal to Israel over their home nations. Catholics have been accused of subversive loyalty to the pope over and against their countries. Now Muslims bear the brunt of nativist antipathy. In Trump's America, both xenophobic sentiment and overt racism became more public and more widely impactful on Muslims in the United States. The interpretive framework I have described here is vulnerable to Trump's rhetoric because both are concerned with the way America *should* be. Conservative evangelicals did not necessarily support all of Trump's policy ideas, nor did they relish the more scandalous details of his personal life. But when parts of his vision and theirs coincided, their bond solidified. Though Trump did not fit these interviewees' definitions of a devout Christian, his engagement with their interpretive framework was key for many a conservative evangelical supporter. Trump may not have always acted the right way as president, but he interpreted the right way for many evangelical Christians, and that indicated a solid understanding of the way the world works. Even while exposed to the rich diversity, complexity, and contradictions of the United States and Islam, Trump and these interviewees asserted that each was built around its own single, unalterable truth.

CHAPTER FIVE

RACIALIZING AND CRIMINALIZING MUSLIMS, 2016[126]

Sarah Beth Kaufman

Racialization and Criminalization of Muslims

In conducting the interviews that resulted in *To Be Honest,* we talked with people from across political and religious spectrums in order to capture a diverse range of experiences prompted by Trump's proposed Muslim ban. This chapter illuminates two sets of very different experiences that I argue are in fact part of a singular process called *criminalization.* In *To Be Honest,* the characters Patrick, Jay, Betty, and Karen are non-Muslims who speak about Muslims as a dangerous, homogenous racial group. Hari, Joshua, and Khadijah are characters who illustrate the impact of such talk, speaking of some of their experiences of subjugation and liberation. As this chapter describes, their positions echo other moments of racialization and criminalization in the late-modern United States.

Background: Studying Race and Criminality

Race and criminality might seem like strange concepts to begin a chapter about Islam, as well they should. Islam is not a race, but a religion. Nearly one quarter of the human population identify as Muslim, and these 1.8 billion people live around the globe, in South Asia and the Middle East-North African region, but also in Europe, the Americas, and sub-Saharan Africa. The estimated 3.5 million Muslims who live in the United States are as racially diverse as the world population. American Muslims describe themselves as white, (30%), Black (23%), Asian (21%), Hispanic (6%), and other or mixed race (19%).[127] Yet the construction of Muslims as a homogenous, dangerous group is not surprising for critical scholars of race and criminality. As Angela Davis wrote, crime discourse is "one of the masquerades behind which 'race,' with all its menacing ideological complexity, mobilizes old public fears and creates new ones." When media and political figures talk of Islam as synonymous with terrorist violence, they access an idea that is foundational to Western civilization. The colonial distinction between dangerous "Black" natives and civilized "white" people created the belief that danger is innate to Blackness.[128]

The U.S. is late to mainstream discrimination against Muslims compared to Europe.[129] Muslims immigrated to the United States in large numbers after 1965 and are well-off compared to other immigrant groups. Yet anti-Muslim hatred is the U.S. is undeniable in the twenty-first century: Muslims and those perceived to be Muslim encounter racial taunts, targeted surveillance, and harassment as part of their everyday lives.[130] This has prompted scholars to describe Muslims as experiencing *racialization*, a historical period during which a "previously racially unclassified group" begins to be viewed as having racial commonalities.[131] For social scientists, racialization is a thing to be accomplished, taking shape in a particular time and place. Racial identity impacts everyday experiences in the United States, from schooling and employment to healthcare and romance: those perceived to be "white" are given advantages compared to people perceived to be "of color." Yet science has shown that race is not biological: a given "white" person might have more shared genetic material with a "Black" person than others who share their racial label. But science does not stop some from making assumptions about racial commonalities. Indeed Hari, Joshua, and Khadijah give voice to aspects of this experience, as I discuss below.

Racial categorizations are historically tied to, but distinct from, the process of criminalization. In the United States, for example, east Asians are considered a racial group but are rarely stereotyped as dangerous.[132] Criminalization is defined by a social group's shift into a category of problems to be solved using the logic and structure of state crime control.[133] Governments are prime actors in this process, and there is little doubt that Muslims have suffered through such treatment by actors representing the American state, especially in the wake of 9/11. As Saher Selod[134] and others have documented, Muslims have been targeted for surveillance on city streets, have been given detention with little evidence, and have received enhanced punishments in prisons. Sharene Razack describes this as Muslims having been veritably "cast out" from Western legal systems following 9/11, excluded from everyday governance in multiple instances.

But state actors do not operate in a vacuum. Criminalization relies on the circulation of beliefs and ideas through the general public. Experts and interest groups in prime social locations—Howard Becker calls them "moral entrepreneurs"—supply frames that successfully resonate in media, political, and public discourse in service of criminalization. Muslims in the United States have become the purview of such entrepreneurs: right-wing Christian and secular organizations have positioned Muslims as a problem to be solved.[135] The media also portray Muslims as potential terrorists, part of what Morgan and Poynting argue is the construction of Muslims as "transnational folk devils"[136] in Western media and political discourse. Less is known about how *everyday* Americans criminalize Muslims, and it is this that our research demonstrates.

To Be Honest showcases the experiences involved with the criminalization process, from the perspectives of both those who criminalize, and those who are criminalized. As I detail, Muslims are criminalized by rhetoric that positions them as a homogenous, threatening population on the one hand, and in need of state crime control measures on the other. In turn, Muslims and people who are mistakenly thought to be Muslim experience fear of unfamiliar spaces and violent encounters. This places Muslims alongside Black and Hispanic American populations who have suffered the brunt of mass incarceration's brutality. Our interviews suggest that despite mainstream rhetoric touting criminal justice reform and post-racial politics, racialization and criminalization are shifting rather than fading away.

Fearing Islam: Karen, Jay, Patrick, and Betty

In Episode 13, the character of Karen turns suddenly to Myra and Ellen, whom she has been sitting with, and tells them that she has a "completely different point of view about Muslims" from them. Despite not being a "crazed

Trump person," as she puts it, Karen tells Myra and Ellen that she thinks Muslim culture "sucks," giving evidence of the human disregard she witnessed while living in rural Pakistan. The interviewee who Karen represents continued along this line as a member of her focus group, telling others that she thought it was "naïve of Americans to think that Muslims are 99% peaceful," and that all Americans should be grappling with a major question: "What does a tolerant society do with an intolerant element?" Despite identifying as politically liberal, this part of Karen's story is an example of what scholars call "reasonable racism" in the "post-racial era."[137] Karen ascribes the objectionable differences that she observes in a foreign land to a notion of enduring Muslim "culture," failing to consider the possibility that she witnessed a more complex intersection of influences. Karen, like most people located in the subjectivity of their own position, is unable to discern the potentially endless geopolitical factors that may have created the moments she remembers. She may have encountered an extreme among local cultures, or a particular segment of the community that would be contradicted by another. The "intolerance" of women's autonomy Karen witnesses, furthermore, may be an unrecognizable concept to those she judges; it is very difficult for Americans, who emphasize the importance of individuality, to accept as morally neutral an overriding concern for religious norms.

Karen represents a broader phenomenon we observed among our interviewees. She and others condemned racism, but nonetheless use language that reflects their fear of an imagined group of homogenous outsiders called Muslim. Samuel and Marley are a self-described white, liberal couple who had been delegates for the Democratic Party. When interviewed about Islam and the presidential campaign, Marley said that Trump's Muslim ban was a "racist-based ideology working through our immigration policies." They then took turns listing minority groups who had likewise been singled out in American history: "Jews were treated like that. The Irish . . . the Japanese Americans, after bombing Pearl Harbor . . . slavery from Africa . . . " But Samuel then clarified his position, saying he was looking for the government to do more to assure Muslims with the potential for terrorist violence were not admitted to the U.S. He told the interviewer:

> I think we should expect our government to do things more expertly when they get into something. Vetting people. I wouldn't want a Nazi sympathizer or a former Nazi still practicing his viewpoints allowed to come in without normal vetting.

Samuel wonders whether immigrant "vetting" is strong enough to flush out potential terrorists. He evokes the metaphor of Nazi sympathizers as an explanation for a threat emanating from Islam. He wonders whether the government should do *something more* to assure that Muslims seeking entrance into the country are not in fact dangerous. Indeed, the language of "vetting" and border security was raised in a full dozen of the interviews and focus groups we conducted. Charles, a Hispanic, Catholic Democrat in his mid-60s, suggested additional policing measures. When asked if he thought the police should be implementing a "stop and frisk" policy, he responded: "I'm all for frisking Muslims, no matter what!" Leaving a concern for civil liberties behind, Charles also does not realize that identifying Muslims by sight is an impossibility, as Muslims are as racially and ethnically diverse as any world religion. Part of the play's work then, is to demonstrate that people who think of themselves as politically progressive, and even anti-racist, can have a blind spot when it comes to Islam. Mondon and Winter describe this as a type of "liberal" Islamophobia that circulates in U.S. media and politics.[138]

This "liberal" racism has important historical context. In the "solutions" posed by Samuel and Charles, one hears echoes of liberal rhetoric from a different era. From the "War on Drugs" to the crackdown on illegal immigration, policing and punishing Black and Hispanic people in the United States has been supported not only by conservatives but also some liberals. Popular initiatives such as President Bill Clinton's Anti-Terrorism bill increased militarization of local and border policing, and neighborhood associations' "National Night Out," targets racial minorities, whether intentionally or not. People from all political persuasions describe this as an "unfortunate consequence" of the project of American security.[139] Our respondents are part of this tradition.

Other characters in the play represent a more unabashed type of anti-Muslim positioning. Jay, Patrick, and Betty embody aspects of the anti-Muslim views that were isolated in "fringe" political groups in the U.S. until well after 9/11 but were heard widely in Trump's national campaign. In Episode 8, "Debating Islam," Jay says in no uncertain terms that Muslims are here "to take over the country." Their "hope and dream" is for the "Islamic flag" to be "flying over the White House instead of the flag of the United States of America." The notion of an imaginary "Islamic flag" is indicative of this group's position: Islam is not to be thought of as one of a series of Judeo-Christian American religions, but more like the political philosophy of a state flying a symbolic banner. The interviewee from which Jay's character is drawn expanded upon this. He said that Muhammed, Islam's founder, was like Karl Marx. Both originated philosophies that risked the safety of the United States. The difference between the two, "Jay" told the interviewer, was that "Marx didn't find a religion to be able to hang his hat on," but "Muhammed did and it was a very smart, smart strategy." Muslims, therefore, like people suspected of Marxist or Leninist sympathies, should be targets of mass enquiry to protect the security of the United States, he argued. Jay's position constructs Islam as a dangerous ideology, as singular and identifiable as that of a lone philosopher, and as worthy of attack as a criminal state. This places Muslims within the purview of the criminal justice system, as a danger to national security.

The takeover will be affected through multiple U.S. institutions, other respondents explained: religion, law, and education. Marty, a retired intelligence officer who also worked for a Christian broadcasting network, told interviewers that Islam is a threat to U.S. Judeo-Christian "culture." The religion was not only *different,* but dangerous. Betty, an Evangelist missionary, elaborated: "Islam is a religion of hate because there is nothing in the Qur'an, not one time ever that they talk about a loving God." A young man recently out of high school admitted that he did not understand the religion exactly, but he knew it was a threat to Americans. He was "not sure if all Islams [sic] believe Americans should be murdered, or if "they believe *all* people who disagree with their beliefs should be murdered," but he concluded, it's giving Islam "a really bad reputation." Together, these three respondents demonstrate a range of potential thinking about the threat of the Islamic religion: it is foreign to the United States' Judeo-Christian culture, based in hate, and poses a direct, deadly threat to "Americans."

Importantly, the threat that respondents describe is both similar to and distinct from the fear of other racialized bodies in the mass incarceration era. Like African Americans and Hispanic migrants, Muslims are spoken about as homogenous, violent, and physically threatening. Yet they are also spoken about as organized, sophisticated, and ideologically-motivated, qualities not previously linked with criminalized Americans. One interviewee explained that Muslims are one of the most serious threats to America's security in history, citing their economic and organizational prowess:

They're highly technical. They're probably the best funded, financed group in the history of groups like that, by taking over other countries with oil fields and things of that nature. They know how to use social media and the internet to propagandize their cause and recruit.

The "take over" of oil fields that this interviewee cites demonstrates the racialization: for him, Arab dominance in world oil production is synonymous with a religious sect. In this sense, Muslim "foreignness" is also evoked. Muslims are people who scheme, gather funding, and take over countries. They could not possibly be American. This language is similar to contemporaneous media scares about "radicalized" Syrian refugees who are feared to be sneaking across the border, or Mexican immigrants invading the southern border.[140]

In Episode 16 of the play, Patrick talks about his fear of Muslims as foreign. "Those people," he says, are different from peaceful Americans:

> We have nothing to do with those people . . . we don't share their politics. We don't share their religion. They need to leave us alone. Why do they want to come over here and bomb us and kill people over here?

Patrick thinks of Muslims as having "nothing to do with" the "us" of which he feels a part. As a 62-year-old white man, his notion of Muslims belies his bias. Americans, for him, are not Muslim in their religion or their politics, which are intrusive and violent. Patrick links his discomfort with foreigners to a concept of the United States rooted in a time before racial insults were censured. He chided another interviewee for saying it wasn't "right" to say that Muslims were dangerous. A "union man" and a Democrat, Patrick was nostalgic for a time when he could simply say what he wanted:

> Back in the days like in the 60s–70s, we didn't have to think about what we were going to say before we said it because you didn't want to hurt nobody's feelings, or didn't want to say the wrong thing . . . Nowadays, you say anything wrong and they take it the wrong way.

Patrick echoes Trump's promise to "make America great again," though he was not sure who he was going to vote for. Regardless, Patrick speaks of Islam as a quality belonging to racialized "others," non-Americans whom he feels are dangerous, and who impinge upon his free speech.

Interviewees like Jay, Karen, or Patrick all pose crime control solutions to the perceived problem of danger. In the play, Barry says this most clearly. He describes himself as a "principled conservative" who worries about Trump being unqualified and potentially damaging to his party. But, Barry says, the country's security is at risk because of the concern with political correctness. In Episode 5, Barry says the country's "hypersensitivity" about race is irrational. Drawing a parallel between critics of Islamophobia and racial profiling, he worries what happens when Americans can't "say something like it was a six-foot Black guy who stole my purse" for fear of being labeled a racist. The interviewee who Barry represents extended this, arguing that targeted scrutiny was necessary to combat Islamic terrorism:

> If there is a phenomenon of radical jihadists that tend to come for the most part from one section of the world, and therefore can be identified physically . . . it doesn't seem to me crazy to understand the threat that way.

The failure to use sight-based profiling, he continues, is "political correctness gone mad." Here Barry explicitly draws together the cases of Black and Muslim profiling. In his view, Black Americans and Muslims are both able to be physically identified and are targeted as threats. Of course, the Muslim religion is no more visible than any other set of beliefs, but even if physical identification was possible, it is unconstitutional to deny civil liberties to Americans on the basis of race and religious identity.

In sum, both "liberal" and conservative respondents imagine Muslims to be a homogenous, non-white racial group with the potential for violence. They describe crime control techniques they think are appropriate to use in defense against Muslims, including targeted "vetting" at the U.S. border and racial profiling within. These are ideas and solutions borrowed from U.S. criminal legal regimes. In a process that DiMaggio and Powell call "institutional isomorphism,"[141] practices developed as part of the build-up of the mass incarceration era are adopted by those who distinguish Muslims as a new threat to Americans' safety. The power of such talk should not be underrated.

Experiences of Subjugation: Hari, Khadijah, and Joshua

During the time that we conducted our interviews, the country was in the midst of a spike in anti-Muslim hate crimes, reaching levels similar to the post-9/11 era.[142] Muslim interviewees who participated in our study, along with the Sikh, Hindu, and self-described Middle Eastern respondents, described being targeted as potential criminals by strangers and acquaintances alike. Sayeeda, a Black Muslim woman in her twenties, described how everyday events can become the site of potential violence. She describes being in the "most diverse Walmart on earth" with her sister when a man in her checkout line behind her picked up his phone. He began loudly talking about terrorists, making clear she and her sister were meant to hear. Sayeeda heard him say: "We should just kill all of them. We just need to go over there and just have a big bomb and kill them all." Because of the danger, her sister urged her to stay quiet even though she wanted to speak up.

An interviewee named Claire converted to Islam as an adult, choosing to wear hijab as part of her religious faith. As a result, she lost her job and became alienated from her family. During the election season, she said her fear was heightened, increasingly scared that someone would "shoot up" her house or run her off the road while she was driving. Growing up a white Christian woman, Claire understood that her choice to wear the hijab on a regular basis removed the protection of her white race that she had previously experienced; she was no longer able to perform whiteness in a way that protected her.

Among the most harrowing experiences in *To Be Honest* were those told by people who were mistakenly thought to be Muslim. In Episode 6, Hari, a Sikh man, tells the audience of the violence he experiences and fears regularly:

> People associated me as Muslim, and I'm not. I get branded in a negative way, just because people don't know, they look at me right away . . . In Oak Creek, Wisconsin, where somebody went into a Sikh temple and started killing because he thought they were Muslims. That's really what happened. He shot nine or ten folks who died. Policemen died, and policemen were injured.

His dilemma is two-fold, because he refuses, in his words, to say: "Hey, don't hate me because I'm not Muslim. I'm a Sikh." For Hari, this would imply that Muslim hatred is okay. He concludes with a wish for a shirt that he could wear to both protect himself and reflect his ethical commitment, one that says, "Don't hate me, I'm a Sikh, but even if I'm a Muslim, still don't hate me." Hari's wife Sarita cries as she describes her fear for her children. They are just as *normal* as other American children, she says. But the turbans mark them as racial outsiders, and they are denied the luxury of experiencing themselves as "normal." Like other racialized Americans, these interviewees describe the frightening impact of the gaze of those who presume, mistakenly, to "know" them and their families. Sayeeda, Claire, Hari, and Sarita's experiences are unified by the ways in which their bodies are read in public. Because Islam is imagined to be a *race*, strangers think they can see their religion—often erroneously—on people they know nothing about.

Joshua's experience in *To Be Honest* illuminates yet another consequence of the racialization and criminalization of Muslims. In Episode 12, he describes how Malcolm X's writing illustrates his own experience. As a Black man, he says, his religious identity is hidden:

> Malcolm X used to say that they don't kill you because you are a Muslim, they don't kill you because you are Christian, protestant, or Jew. They kill you because you are Black. The Powers That Be could care less that I am calling myself a Muslim. All they look at is the dark skin. That is how I am judged, that is how we are all judged, as Black people.

Joshua has not experienced himself as targeted because of his Muslim faith, in other words. He has been targeted because he is Black. Regardless of his religious faith, his perceived racial identity dominates the way he is treated. In his interview, Joshua describes his experience of conversion, of becoming a Muslim. He became a member of the Nation of Islam after reading Malcolm X and wanting to be immersed in the critique of racialized violence. This conversion meant a change in the way that he carried himself, conducted himself in public, and thought of himself. Being a Muslim meant that he had to "clean up" inside and out, as he told us. But in public spaces in the U.S., that transformation was invisible to those who saw him only as *Black*. His religious identity was eclipsed by his race.

Muslims in America are imagined to belong to a single racial category, and Joshua does not fit this perception. His *Blackness* misidentifies him as non-Muslim just as Claire's *whiteness* misidentifies her until she puts on the hijab. As Habiba Noor details in this volume, this racial imaginary is a historically rooted one, shaped not only by the orientalist imperialism of the eighteenth and nineteenth centuries, but also the twentieth and twenty-first centuries perceived relationship to Muslims across the world.

Discussion and Conclusion

Although Muslims have been framed as outsiders in the United States since its founding, *To Be Honest* shows how Trump's so-called "Muslim ban" thrust the question of being Muslim into the forefront of public consciousness. Muslims are constructed as both foreign and familiar—rooted in the well-known racial stratification of the United States—yet alien in their cultural and ideological identity. The particular method of vilification is molded by the U.S.'s long history of criminalization of Black and Hispanic people. Our respondents assume that they can *see religion* on the bodies of people in the public sphere, just as race has been constructed to be phenotypically identifiable. Joining Hispanic and Black Americans then, Muslims are talked about as inhabiting dangerous bodies in the public sphere.

This demonstrates both the relevance and the mutability of "fear of crime" beliefs in the twenty-first century. Although the mass incarceration of racialized Americans is declining according to some, our research supports others in suggesting that criminalization is mutating rather than diminishing. As Christian hegemony continues to decline in the U.S., sociologists who study crime, race, and religion should use the conceptual tools of criminalization to interrogate Muslim subjugation on the one hand; and gain insight from groups who have resisted such subjugation on the other.

CHAPTER SIX

PERFORMANCE AND THE DANGERS OF REPRESENTATION: A CONVERSATION

Sarah Beth Kaufman and Tahir Naqvi

In the tradition of Mahatma Gandhi, who creates a false Socratic dialogue in the form of an interview to describe his concept of *Hind Swaraj*, or Home Rule, the following is a created conversation between Sarah Beth Kaufman, a sociologist and one of the authors of the script *To Be Honest*, and Tahir Naqvi, an anthropologist and one of the play's actors. This format best captures the unusual positions of scholar-playwright-subject (Kaufman) and scholar-actor-subject (Naqvi) that characterized our work for this project. Through writing and talking with each other and sharing our conversation here, we formalize our own experiences with representation and ethics, and invite others to think it through with us.

KAUFMAN: So, tell me about your experience participating in our play. You said it was meaningful in a way that you found interesting.

NAQVI: The play is meaningful in a lot of ways, but if I were to think about myself personally . . . I'm a Muslim American of South Asian heritage who performed as a Sikh American character. He is a husband, a father, a middle-aged man, who, unlike me, emigrated as an adult to the United States from India. With that said, I'm from the same part of the world that many Sikhs hail from, Punjab, and I've written on the communal genocide that took place there following the 1947 partition of India. In order to do the role, I had to think about what I needed to bring to that little slice of dialogue you included in the play. I drew on my sense of history and my more recent experiences in San Antonio as a Muslim. I know the region of Punjab and its history, and I know something about the way Sikhs are targeted in a very peculiar way in the United States. And yet it was clear that I needed more than this. All of it came together for me in a moment that I remember vividly. It was the day before the first performance, and I went to a Sikh temple that afternoon to learn how to tie the pagri . . . the Sikh turban. I eventually had to have it tied by someone else because it requires a complex set of movements. I realized that the pagri is not simply something that one throws on in any context. And the amount of time it took to put it on gave me ample time to realize the nature of the transformation I was undertaking. There was a young man from the community there that afternoon who helped me. It was kind of like I had my hair done, and that was it. But then I realized that I needed to drive my car home wearing this turban.

KAUFMAN: I didn't know that.

NAQVI: Yes, it was very intense. I got to experience in real time the anxiety of being physically and publicly marked by one's faith. This was part of my realization of the character of Hari: anxiety and its everyday embodiment was part of his normal existence. As an actor, I began to think that this is the moment where the strength of one's convictions must enter into the way you concretely embody a social space. Transforming fear, possibly even anxiety itself, into something like vigilance and concern. The constancy of concern. I don't have anything like that in my personal biography. Personally, I don't present in public space as Muslim, despite the fact that I have a beard. So by the end of it all, I'm driving home and I'm thinking, "This is intense." I realized this concern and vigilance is something that Sikh men in America must also negotiate as a stance, especially if one has a family and sons.

KAUFMAN: You just said something that I didn't quite understand. One, you said you don't pass as a Muslim? But you are Muslim, and you are brown.

NAQVI: In America and Europe, at least, I think Muslims are marked as much by how they *choose* to appear, in the name of adherence for their faith, as they are by their ethnic and racial appearance. In the United States, for instance, one might not "look" Muslim until they don certain types of dress, such as the hijab, or, for men, a longer beard. Crucially, none of these outward characteristics of Muslimness are as apparent as what a Sikh man has to display out of obligation to his faith.

               That's the second part of the character, right? Aside from the negotiated quality of their existence, there is the irreversibility of their turban. Sikh men are often mistaken for Muslims and face harassment in public as a result. Aside from the question of vigilance, then, is the question of how one is to respond to this harassment in an ethical fashion. Should they allow themselves to be mistaken for Muslim or should they correct those who jeer, insult, and, on more than a few occasions—assault them? I find the collective hesitation of Sikh men to correct such mischaracterizations about their background and faith to be one of the most potent examples of the concept of grace in contemporary American civil-religious life. Again, we're talking about the choice that so many Sikh men make to *not* correct those who often violently believe them to be someone else.

KAUFMAN: And it is a decision informed by that faith, Hari told us, that he does *not* correct the mistake, does not attempt to secure his own safety by declaring his *actual* religious faith. But in that moment of deciding whether or not to correct the stranger's mistake, there's also an acknowledgment of the commonality between Sikhs and Muslims.

NAQVI: We live in this country together and so there's all these intersecting histories. There's the regional history, the South Asian connection. Muslims and Sikhs killed each other in the tens of thousands during partition. At that time too, physical appearance was part of the way genocidal violence was conducted: the length of hair and beard; the look of one's garb; whether you were circumcised or not. Aside from the power of their faith, there's a specific and ruptured history that underscores the Sikh man's decision to not correct the present. Perhaps it is tied to trauma and the work of repair.

KAUFMAN: The passing and hiding and costuming and checking is part of every colonial and imperial history, isn't it? Though not every instance of racial passing and hiding involves religious as well as ethnic identity. And it doesn't always work the way we think it will. Joshua, in the play, talks about his invisibility as Muslim because he is always perceived as Black. His racial identity in the United States masks his religious identity. In Germany or France, his perceived Blackness would be read differently. Other people we interviewed—Muslims who looked white or Latinx—they also reported that their religious identity was invisible, unless they put on certain clothing that marked them, as you said. And of course there are Arab Christians who are mistakenly targeted as Muslim as well in the United States. At what point in South Asian history did Sikh men try to pass as Muslim in Punjab?

NAQVI: During the genocide of partition in the 1940s. Where millions of people died. It was a civil genocide, like Rwanda during our lifetime.

KAUFMAN: Passing as either Muslim or Hindu would protect them?

NAQVI: Passing as Muslim if you're being attacked by Muslims, or Hindu if attacked by Hindus, both of which were going on during partition. But, as I said, Sikhs also played a role in the genocide against Muslims during partition. They were like a third rail, but a very powerful third rail. They killed a lot of Muslims in the eastern part of Punjab, that's now part of India. Then Muslims did the same to Sikhs in West Punjab. Lahore was a Sikh-majority city. Much of this violence between the various communal groups was imagined as a response. That's how large-scale violence like this works. The Sikhs living in Pakistan at the time of partition fled. They fled or migrated or ran away, or were pushed, depending on who is telling the story. That's the regional history I drew on for the character in the play. It helped me to account for why Hari, like so many Sikhs, must grapple with what response to give when he is (mis)seen as Muslim. What I mean is this: it would be so simple for Sikhs in America to turn the past—the violations of partition—into a reason to disavow Muslims in America today. And yet that's not what happens. There's something at work, there's this thing, it's beyond liberal civility, it's something that, it's not even . . . it's an *act* of some kind, obviously.

KAUFMAN: One of the Sikh men we interviewed described it as self-respect, respect for Muslims as self-respect.

NAQVI: By being mistaken for the "other," you're put in this situation of having to maintain a kind of *regard* for the "other." An "other" that, in very real and actual ways, stands in your place in the moment of racial violence. It's, as you noted, a form of self-respect.

KAUFMAN: They told us that the choice is driven by their religious principles. A commitment to humanity as a religious impetus.

NAQVI: There is some relationship to the principles of the religion, but history is important too. Today's relationship is different. There might even be gestures of remorse involved in Hari's refusal to deny he is Muslim. All kinds of things could be at stake.

KAUFMAN: Yeah.

NAQVI: But the fear I felt when I drove home from the gurdwara [Sikh place of worship] was definitely a thing.

KAUFMAN: We interviewed Hindu South Asians who were profiled as Muslim. In retelling those moments, they described themselves as fearful. From our Sikh interviewees, the sentiment was more defiant, perhaps, and sad. But then again, this difference could have been about gender, now that I think of it. The South Asian interviewees were both women, and the Sikh interviewees I was thinking of were both men. Their retelling could also be about masculinity.

NAQVI: You could make that argument. You could say yes, there's this culture of being a man. There's a kind of masculine, militant, political cosmology among Sikhs in India and in the diaspora that is part of their self-construction as a marginalized nation and religious community within India. Still, Sikh *political* masculinity is not this thing that runs unimpeded through history. But, yes, there is a connection to the notion of honor, a very gendered category in South Asia. Courage and honor are definitely a powerful part of the Sikh ethos. I mean, the idea of not being weak, weak enough to deny that one is Muslim . . . your self-respect hinges on *not* denying that you're someone who you are not. It's a complex articulation of morality, identity, and power.

            Sikhs do what's known as *seva*, service work, in places precisely where they know they will stand out. They're really out there. They go to Syria. They're doing humanitarian work there. Part of their commitment to service is wound up with their commitment to being courageous. It puts them out there in a way that says that they're not going to be cowed by public impressions of who they are or who they might be.

KAUFMAN: From what I understand, the complicated recognition between Sikhs and Muslims in the U.S. is something that you came to think deeply about not as part of your scholarship, but because you put on the turban for the play. I'm curious how you experienced the performative aspect of this?

NAQVI: Yeah, I'm not an actor. This was my first time properly trying to get into a character as such. So to prepare I tried thinking about what the character and his wife are trying to get across *together*. Their relationship matters. I really thought about how I would be sitting next to her and the kind of relationship we might embody. She's under Hari's protection. I was not just protecting her but also her emotions. I'm there, but it's her stories that offer the really moving parts of the scene. I'm there just to attest and kind of complete something, right? This brings in the masculinity part again, doesn't it?

KAUFMAN: You had to become a particular type of masculine character.

NAQVI: Yes. Different levels of embodiment. Another factor is that we have a son, and what about him? There's an urgency to that, to this young boy who is also wearing a turban and who needs immediate protection. That feeling of chronic urgency—of vigilance—is what I ultimately came up with, that was the sort of culminating effect that I was thinking of for the character. The character is concerned and urgent, but still very clear about all of it despite all that. He's saying: we're not going to deny who we are by denying that there are also others who are "others." Does that make sense? I realized there's a reason why actors do research. I mean, I came at it in reverse, as a researcher who had to try to become an actor . . . I realized that there's this really fascinating relationship. The moment in the car was a real threshold . . . It was a really acute feeling, because I couldn't take it off (it needed to stay on until the performance).

KAUFMAN: Right.

NAQVI: I had to keep it on. It was not like a hat that they just put on and like, "here you go."

KAUFMAN: It's funny, but you are misrecognized as a part of your daily experience. I don't know if you think about it in those terms. But you are often taken for someone who is Indian and therefore Hindu or at least not Muslim, right? Yet you are actually Muslim. But to really understand what it means to *fear* being targeted as a Muslim, you had to put on the turban of a Sikh. That's some complicated process there. Is that what they call method acting?

NAQVI: There's a lot of unintended ironies here. All of this speaks to the horribly sort of generic way in which, in the U.S. at least, these groups are just sort of *subsumed* under one.

KAUFMAN: I call it racism, and a racism that is specific to the United States. In Western Europe, where so much has been written about the experiences of Islamophobia, there is a different kind of racial history, a different kind of racism. Here, African Americans cannot be imagined to be Muslim, where people who look Arab and even South Asian are.

NAQVI: Yeah, it might also mark you in public as an immigrant or recently arrived. But then there's the public in terms of questioning rights, a political question. What is a Muslim's role? What are a Muslim's civil rights? Muslims connect with other minorities in this sense, the intersections can develop politically. At this political level, I'm very much willing to identify and be identified as a Muslim. Since we live in America, nobody is regulating my religion at a public level anyway, right? Nobody's saying, "Oh, you're a Muslim, therefore you will have this kind of life in this country." You expect when you're walking down the street for people to just leave you be, right? That's the whole promise of living in America. You don't want to be seen as stereotyped, or you want to be free to be who you are, but part of that means people minding their own business. The whole aspect of privacy and anonymity is really very important to all this.

KAUFMAN: One of the themes we set up in the play challenges the simplicity of that notion that America provides the freedom to be who you are. When we juxtapose two views about Islam that are seemingly contradictory, we see that they are both justified by protecting the banner of just this aspect of "Americanism." There are those who say that a core part of America is to separate church from state, keep religion "out of politics," which is part of the dream of being free from harassment, as you say. But another faction argues that Islam is an essential topic for secular politics because it *threatens* the ability to be free in America. Like communism, right, it wants to take over. You can't help but recognize a commonality between these two views in that they are defending freedom. But it brings up really difficult questions about the *concept* of freedom. Freedom as it was imagined at the country's founding was inhabitable only by white Christian men. Have women, African Americans, Jews who now have the right to "freedom," changed the concept to accommodate different types of freedoms, or adjusted to a "freedom" that requires assimilation? It is an enduring question.

NAQVI: Yes, it's sort of like this: I wear the hijab, and you respect my right to wear the hijab. In the same way that you'd ask me to respect your right to your womb. Muslim women activists in France and the U.K. see the clear connection between those things.

KAUFMAN: I haven't heard that here in the U.S. Or at least not in San Antonio, which also complicates the play's perspective. People ask us if this is a *local* play, like because San Antonio is so *Mexican* that it's a problem. It's local, yes, but it's also more. The vastness and diversity of the United States is another aspect of what is represented in the play. All of these voices, sometimes talking to one another, sometimes talking past one another—that too, seems very American. But putting those conversations on stage, without commentary, that seemed very *un*-American to us, or at least un-American in this particular moment in history. It feels so rare these days to hear different perspectives without some sort of moderating ruler that decides who is *right*.

NAQVI: That second night of performing *To Be Honest*, we got the help of GP Singh, who is a wonderful, longtime member of the San Antonio community, an entrepreneur, and a national-level leader in the Sikh community. My co-character, who was playing my wife, was able to get him involved to help us with the second performance. He came and brought someone to actually wrap the turban properly. GP saw the whole show and has become a real advocate for the performances of *To Be Honest*. All the different forms of acknowledgment taking place that evening was something else too. It was about the city and making something happen, constructing a kind of close relationship, not intimate in the traditional sense but definitely not abstract. It was one of those important face-to-face moments that solidified for me what life in San Antonio could be like.

KAUFMAN: Yes, that is what we were most hoping for by making the interviews into something that would be *performed*. In the super-mediated world we live in, the theater is such a demanding venue in terms of embodiment and recognition. The audience is impacted, of course, but we became aware of how much the actors also experienced, and that wasn't something we were expecting. On our website, there are some clips of some of the actors being interviewed, and we were really moved by the ways they describe embodying the interviewees, and how it transformed their understanding of those they were representing. Tell me what was exchanged, you think, in that moment with GP.

NAQVI: We all realized we were from the same part of the world. We were speaking in Hindi. I understand Punjabi, but I don't speak it. It was that sense that we're from a part of the world where if I were instead, let's say, an Arab man or a Latino man playing a Sikh man, I don't think that moment would have been the same.

KAUFMAN: Maybe they wouldn't have even come to wrap the turban. It's an extremely trusting act. Maybe they trusted you to represent the character not only because of your politics or that you are a scholar, but that you could literally remember—and therefore reproduce the image of—the ways in which Sikh men are both *at home* in South Asia and *away from home* here in the United States. There is a commensurability in your experiences in that way.

NAQVI: I took pictures of myself before the performance day and I don't think I would be offending anyone by saying that I really look like a Sikh man! I think you guys had asked me to not shave my beard and keep it long, which I did. It was really long in that performance.

KAUFMAN: We should include that here, if we can find it.

NAQVI: In becoming Hari, I really felt there was this kind of reverse process of regard and disguise, a possibility in the moment of performance for a certain exchange between two *actual* people. This is where the documentary character of your play comes into the equation. Hari and I are truly connected to each other through our shared regional histories, and also here, in America, through the strange potential we share for being mistaken for each other. The Sikh community's trust in me and my performance was, in this sense, a continuation of their self-regard, while my performance that night really was an attempt to practice a kind of reciprocity.

KAUFMAN: Did you talk about this with them, during the thing? Did you acknowledge it?

NAQVI: No, this is all my thinking, putting it together now, after the fact.

KAUFMAN: When it was happening, there wasn't any shared look or signal?

NAQVI: There was just warmth. I felt really grateful in a way that wasn't sappy. So I wouldn't say I was aware of all the things I'm telling you now, but they might have been moving in me in that sense. It was emotional but it was not some emotion that needed to be resolved or put out there as something.

KAUFMAN: I'm sorry to take us away from that shared warmth, but I can't help but think about the inverse. I mean, it is such a different experience of putting on blackface, you know? And part of what I'm thinking about is the ethics of representation. Why was it okay for us to ask you to adopt what might be thought of as different racial characteristics? How can religious or ethnic or racial representation be anti-racist when it has so much in common with that old, racist performative practice?

NAQVI: This is about history and what it means to live in the shadow of large-scale events. Whether it's partition or 9/11—events have really powerful habitations and traces in everyday life. Here I'm really drawing on Veena Das and what she has to say about this in her book, *Life and Words*.

KAUFMAN: Yes, we can see how history is present in these moments when one has no choice but to be involved, to take a position. I think that's what we learned in conducting the interviews. The 2016 election was one of these moments when crisis and non-crisis collapse, when the public's involvement in the issue of Islam was much deeper than we anticipated. It seemed odd at first that literally everyone we spoke to—save for two people who were generally incoherent—was passionately involved in the questions we were asking. That's not usual for a scholarly study. But the issue seemed *personal* to so many different kinds of people. The personal and the political were inseparable, which I guess is the point, but it was also a surprise.

NAQVI: The play itself feels like an intervention and a symptom of a certain late liberal moment. It's trying to articulate something like a liberal possibility, by bringing together these voices who are speaking in this public-private setting of an interview, who are partly confiding in you and partly just performing their free subjectivity as free people who believe they have the right to say what they want. To offer their opinion, right?

KAUFMAN: Though we also cheated, right? We created a safe environment, tried to obey some racial rules of recognition, that I as a Jew didn't interview Muslims and Habiba as a Muslim didn't interview the Islamophobes. So what does that mean for honest representation? What parts of our interviewees are we representing when we create these conditions for them?

NAQVI: What if you hadn't played racial politics and then incorporated interviewees' very stilted and incoherent attempts to sound politically correct? That would have been interesting too. I'm just saying that there's all these elements that are informing this play broadly that are part of this crisis moment, where liberalism is speaking from some sense that its foundations are not secure. I think these are real questions for artists and art right now.

KAUFMAN: We—the playwrights—aren't artists, you know? So that's also why I find all of this interesting. Are our (social scientists') ethics of representation different from what theirs (artists') might be? How disciplinary are we when it comes to racial violence? I suspect that the answer is much like the genetic makeup of racial categorization itself. There's more variation within so-called "races" and "disciplines" than between them. I think there's a lot to be learned about the ways in which performers and artists think about theatrical representation. Another element of collapse in late modernity is the collapse between aesthetics and morality, right? I mean, there is no more apolitical art, and certainly not apolitical art that claims to represent an experience that isn't the author's.

NAQVI: And here we have to talk about the collapse of the concept of tolerance too.

KAUFMAN: Wendy Brown talks about this as a problematic concept to begin with. Who wants to be tolerated? She calls it "Regulating Aversion."

NAQVI: Alternatively, a liberal response to being mistaken for an oppressed minority might take the following form: "In fact I'm not Jewish. I may look Jewish to you, but I'm actually Protestant, but I want to let you know that what you said to me was still very racist." That would be a liberal, political response. Because there's this overarching commitment to, and attachment to, the *truth* as something governing my relationship to . . .

KAUFMAN: Ethics.

NAQVI: To ethics. Exactly. But in Trump's case, his attachment is to something else, right? What is that thing?

KAUFMAN: Do both of these have to do with masculinity? The Sikh refusal to perform tolerance I read as part of the masculine imperative for honor and courage. Is there a kind of masculinity in Trump's game of refusing liberal ethics? And what is the Jew to do in all this? My own involvement in this process is almost as multifaceted as yours. I didn't understand my own political identity as so wrapped up in Judaism until I had to be clear about what kind of Jew I am, given all of the anti-Muslim sentiment. For me, Judaism was always political activism, anti-racist activism, because of the type of Judaism my grandparents practiced as lefties in New York. Then I come down to San Antonio and I couldn't imagine staking claims in this debate. Yet here we are. What do you think about that? What does a Muslim playing a Sikh misidentified as a Muslim make of a Jewish co-author?

NAQVI: There is something particularly tribal about life in San Antonio. It's very hard to be seen as an ethnically unmarked individual here. Why and how that happens, is perhaps for another time and another play!

KAUFMAN: Right. It's the trust among friends that alleviates the potential violence, isn't it? Not the other way around?

NAQVI: Maybe.

APPENDIX A: INTERVIEW GUIDE

ENGAGEMENT QUESTIONS

1) Tell me a little about yourself . . . anything you think is important.
2) Where do you get your news?

POLITICAL RHETORIC

3) In the Presidential campaign, a lot has been said about Islam. What have you heard?
   a. Are these issues being talked about in your social network?
   b. When was the last time you heard a conversation about Islam?
   c. Why do you think Islam is an issue in the campaign?
   d. How much has the campaign affected your thinking?

ATTITUDE QUESTIONS

4) Does this discussion around Islam remind you of any other political conversation in history?

#5, 6 and 7 IF NECESSARY:
5) Do you remember hearing about this story? A few weeks ago, young man had boarded a plane on Southwest Airlines when he was overheard speaking Arabic on the phone. A passenger alerted a crew member, and the young man was escorted off the plane and not allowed to fly. It was later confirmed that he was a U.S. citizen with no links to any terrorist organization. How would you feel if you witnessed this?
6) And do you remember this? A young couple, one American-born and the other Pakistan-born, shoot up a room full of people in San Bernardino, California, killing 14 and injuring 28 others. The FBI calls them "homegrown terrorists," motivated by sympathy with extremist Islamic groups. They were not shown to have any official ties to terrorist groups. Do you think this is different from other mass shootings in the U.S.?
7) There is an argument that the police in the United States should be able to "stop and frisk" people they find suspicious. What do you think of this policy and would you support a similar policy for Muslims?

PERSONAL HISTORY QUESTION

8) I'm curious about how you've formulated your ideas about Islam.
   a. Do you know any Muslims?

b. Can you remember how old you were when you first heard about Islam talked about in politics?

c. Has your (education, church group, social group) been influential?

d. How do your opinions compare to your parents' or other (community groups or the nation)?

9) Have you ever experienced fear around these issues?

EXIT QUESTION

10) Is there anything else I should have asked you or you would like to tell us about Islam or the election?

APPENDIX B:
QUESTIONS FOR AUDIENCE AND ACTOR ENGAGEMENT

1) What are your thoughts about the performance?
2) Did you hear any voices that sounded familiar? What were they?
3) Did you hear any voices that shared perspectives that you hadn't heard before?
4) What would you say is the overall message of the performance?

BIBLIOGRAPHY

Abrams, Courtney, Karen Albright, and Aaron Panofsky. "Contesting the New York Community: From Liminality to the 'New Normal' in the Wake of September 11." *City and Community* 3, no. 3 (2004): 189–220.

ACLU. "Timeline of the Muslim Ban." Accessed February 15, 2021. https://www.aclu-wa.org/pages/timeline-muslim-ban.

AFP Getty. "A Woman in a Burkini, a Woman in a Bikini and a Woman in a Swimming Costume on a Beach Near Bizerte." In Romina McGuinness and Alice Foster, "What is the Burkini? Why Have French Towns Banned the Full-Body Swimsuit?" *Express*, August 18, 2016, https://www.express.co.uk/news/world/701626/Burkini-what-is-full-body-swimsuit-Muslim-swimmers-French-ban-towns-France-fine-burka.

Ahmed, Leila. *Women and Gender in Islam: Historical Roots of a Modern Debate.* New Haven: Yale University Press, 1992.

Alimahomed-Wilson, Sabrina. "When the FBI Knocks: Racialized State Surveillance of Muslims." *Critical Sociology* 45, no. 6 (2019): 871–887.

Ali, Wajahat, Eli Clifton, Matthew Duss, Lee Fang, Scott Keyes, and Faiz Shakir. "'Fear, Inc.': The Roots of the Islamophobia Network in America." Washington, D.C.: *Center for American Progress*, August 26, 2011. https://www.americanprogress.org/issues/religion/reports/2011/08/26/10165/fear-inc/.

Allegri, Carlo (Reuters). "Police Forensics Investigators Work on June 12 at the Scene of the Mass Shooting at the Pulse Nightclub in Orlando." In Adam Goldman and Mark Berman, "'They Took Too Damn Long': Inside the Police Response to the Orlando Shooting." *The Washington Post*, August 1, 2016, https://www.washingtonpost.com/world/national-security/they-took-too-damn-long-inside-the-police-response-to-the-orlando-shooting/2016/08/01/67a66130-5447-11e6-88eb-7dda4e2f2aec_story.html.

AP. "Iraqi Security Forces and Civilians Gather at the Site After a Car Bomb Hit Karada, a Busy Shopping District in the Center of Baghdad, Iraq." In Lizzie Dearden, "Baghdad Attack: Death Toll from Isis Bombing Rises to 250 in Deadliest Explosion to Hit Iraq Capital Since 2003." *Independent*, July 6, 2016, https://www.independent.co.uk/news/world/middle-east/baghdad-bombing-attack-latest-news-isis-islamic-state-death-toll-shopping-centre-ramadan-shia-a7122196.html.

Bail, Christopher A. *Terrified: How Anti-Muslim Fringe Organizations Became Mainstream.* Princeton, NJ: Princeton University Press, 2015.

Barthes, Roland. *Image-Music-Text.* Translated by Stephen Heath. New York: Macmillan, 1977.

Bayoumi, Moustafa. "Racing Religion." *CR: The New Centennial Review* 6, no. 2 (2006): 267–293.

Becker, Howard. *Outsiders: Studies in the Sociology of Deviance.* New York, NY: The Free Press, 1963.

Bentley, Eric. *Are You Now or Have You Ever Been?* New York: Samuel French, 1979.

Bexar County Elections Department. "November 8, 2016 Election Totals Report." November 8, 2016. https://www.bexar.org/DocumentCenter/View/9438/November-8-2016-Media-Report.

Bhatia, Aditi, and Christopher Jenks. "Fabricating the American Dream in U.S. Media Portrayals of Syrian Refugees: A Discourse Analytical Study." *Discourse and Communication* 12, no. 3 (2018): 221–239.

Bhatia, Amit A. "American Evangelicals and Islam: Their Perspectives, Attitudes and Practices Towards Muslims in the US," *Transformation: An International Journal of Holistic Mission Studies* 34, no. 1 (2017): 29.

Boal, Augusto. *Theatre of the Oppressed.* New York: Theatre Communications Group, 1985.

Bonilla-Silva, Eduardo. 2014. *Racism Without Racists: Color-Blind Racism and the Persistence of Racial Inequality in the United States, 4th ed.* Lanham, MD: Rowman & Littlefield.

Braunstein, Ruth. "Muslims as Outsiders, Enemies, and Others: The 2016 Presidential Election and the Politics of Religious Exclusion." *American Journal of Cultural Sociology* 5, no. 3 (2017): 362–363.

Brecht, Bertolt. *Brecht on Theatre.* Translated by John Willett. New York: Hill and Wang, 1964.

Brown, Wendy. *Regulating Aversion: Tolerance in the Age of Identity and Empire.* Princeton, NJ. Princeton University Press, 2006.

Bulliet, Richard W. *The Case for Islamo-Christian Civilization.* New York: Columbia University Press, 2006.

Bush, George W. "Backgrounder: The President's Quotes on Islam." *The White House.* Accessed February 15, 2021. https://georgewbush-whitehouse.archives.gov/infocus/ramadan/islam.html.

Cainkar, Louise. *Homeland Insecurity: The Arab American and Muslim American Experience After 9/11.* New York, NY: Russell Sage Foundation, 2009.

Carroll, Lauren, and Louis Jacobson. "Trump Cites Shaky Survey in Call to Ban Muslims from Entering US." *Politifact,* December 9, 2015. https://www.politifact.com/factchecks/2015/dec/09/donald-trump/trump-cites-shaky-survey -call-ban-muslims-entering/.

Casanova, José. "Immigration and the New Religious Pluralism: A European Union/United States Comparison." In *Democracy and the New Religious Pluralism,* edited by Thomas Banchoff, 59–84. New York: Oxford, 2007.

Cesari, Jocelyne. *Why the West Fears Islam: An Exploration of Muslims in Liberal Democracies.* New York, NY: Palgrave Macmillan, 2013.

Channel 4 News. "Sanders pays tribute to Muhammad Ali," *Channel 4 News,* June 5, 2016. https://www.facebook.com /watch/?v=10153796081356939.

Cimino, Richard. "'No God in Common:' American Evangelical Discourse on Islam after 9/11." *Review of Religious Research* 47, no. 2 (2005): 162–174.

CNN. "#notinmyname: Fighting Extremism." *CNN,* September 18, 2014. https://www.cnn.com/2014/09/18/world /gallery/not-in-my-name/index.html.

CNN. "Transcript: CNN Presidential Town Hall: America's Military and The Commander and Chief." *CNN Press Room,* September 28, 2016. https://cnnpressroom.blogs.cnn.com/2016/09/28/transcript-cnn-presidential-town-hall -americas-military-and-the-commander-and-chief/.

Coleridge, Samuel Taylor. *Biographia Literaria.* Edited by Adam Roberts. Edinburgh: Edinburgh University Press, 2014.

Condon, Frank, and Ron Sossi. *The Chicago Conspiracy Trial: A Theatrical Arrangement of the Original Trial Transcripts.* New York: Theatre Communications Group, 1979.

C-SPAN. "Clip of Presidential Candidate Donald Trump Rally in Mount Pleasant, South Carolina." *C-SPAN,* December 7, 2015. https://www.c-span.org/video/?c4566084/user-clip-donald-trummp-ban-muslim.

C-SPAN. "Debate on 'Radical Islam' and Terrorism." *C-SPAN,* June 28, 2016. https://www.c-span.org/video/?411887-1 /hearing-examines-use-term-radical-islam-terrorism-fight.

Das, Veena. *Life and Words: Violence and the Descent into the Ordinary.* Oakland, CA: University of California Press, 2006.

Davis, Angela. "Race and Criminalization." In *The House that Race Built,* edited by Wahneema Lubiano, 264–275. New York, NY: Vintage Books, 1997.

Demir, Nilufer (AFP/Getty Images), "A Turkish Paramilitary Police Officer Carries the Body of 2-year-old Syrian Refugee Alan Kurdi, Found Washed Ashore Near the Turkish Resort of Bodrum in September 2015." In Diane Cole, "Following Up: The Aunt Of The Drowned Syrian Boy Tells What Happened After The Tragedy." *National Public Radio,* August 31, 2018, https://www.npr.org/sections/goatsandsoda/2018/08/31/642952840/an-aunts -memoir-remembering-the-drowned-syrian-boy-on-the-beach

DiMaggio, Paul, and Walter Powell. "The Iron Cage Revisited: Institutional Isomorphism and Collective Rationality in Organizational Fields." *American Sociological Review* 48, no. 2 (1983): 147–160.

Edwards, Derek, and Alessandra Fasulo. "'To Be Honest': Sequential Uses of Honesty Phrases in Talk-In-Interaction." *Research on Language and Social Interaction* 39, no. 4 (2006): 343–376.

Emerson, Michael, and Christian Smith. *Divided by Faith: Evangelical Religion and the Problem of Race in America.* New York, NY: Oxford University Press, 2000.

Fairclough, Norman. "Critical Discourse Analysis." In *How to Analyse Talk in Institutional Settings: A Casebook of Methods*, edited by A. McHoul and M. Rapley, 25–38. London: Continuum, 2001.

Fanon, Frantz. *Black Skin, White Masks.* New York, NY: Grove Press, 1952 [1967].

Fenton, Elizabeth. *Religious Liberties: Anti-Catholicism and Liberal Democracy in Nineteenth-Century U.S. Literature and Culture.* Oxford: Oxford University Press, 2011.

Flanagan, Hallie. *Arena: The History of the Federal Theatre.* New York: Benjamin Blom, 1940.

Gambino, Lauren, and Madhvi Pankhania. "How We Got Here: A Complete Timeline of 2016's Historic US Election." *The Guardian*, November 8, 2016. https://www.theguardian.com/us-news/2016/nov/07/us-election-2016 -complete-timeline-clinton-trump-president.

Getty Images. "Bernie Sanders Described Himself as a 'Bit of a Boxing' Fan as He Paid Tribute to Muhammad Ali." In Robert Costa, "Bernie Sanders Pays Tribute to Muhammad Ali for 'Courageous' Opposition to Vietnam War." *Independent*, June 5, 2016. https://www.independent.co.uk/news/people/muhammad-ali-dead-bernie-sanders-tribute -vietnam-war-us-election-a7066296.html.

GhaneaBassiri, Kambiz. "Islamophobia and American History: Religious Stereotyping and Out-Grouping of Muslims in the United States." In *Islamophobia in America: The Anatomy of Intolerance*, edited by Carl W. Ernst, 53–74. New York: Palgrave Macmillan, 2013.

Gomez, Michael A. "Muslims in Early America." *The Journal of Southern History* 60, no. 4 (1994): 671–710.

Green, Todd. "By Any Other Name: Why the 'Travel Ban' Really Is a Muslim Ban," *Religion News Service*, July 3, 2018. https://religionnews.com/2018/07/03/by-any-other-name-why-the-travel-ban-really-is-a-muslim-ban/.

Green, Todd H. *The Fear of Islam: An Introduction to Islamophobia in the West.* Minneapolis: Augsburg Fortress Publishers, 2015.

Guerra, Kristine. "Calif. Attackers Assault Sikh Man, Removed His Turban, Cut Off His Hair." *NDTV*, October 10, 2016. https://www.ndtv.com/indians-abroad/calif-attackers-assault-sikh-man-removed-his-turban-cut-off-his-hair-1472310.

Gunter, Joel. "Trump's 'Muslim Lockdown': What is the Center for Security Policy?" *BBC News*, December 8, 2015. https://www.bbc.com/news/world-us-canada-35037943.

Habermas, Jürgen. *The Structural Transformation of the Public Sphere: An Inquiry into a Category of Bourgeois Society.* Translated by Thomas Burger. Cambridge, Massachusetts: MIT Press, 1989.

Huntington, Samuel P. "The Clash of Civilizations?" In *Culture and Politics: A Reader*, edited by Lane Crothers and Charles Lockhart, 99–118. New York: Palgrave Macmillan, 2000.

Jamal, Amaney, and Nadine Naber, eds. *Race and Arab Americans Before and After 9/11: From Invisible Citizens to Visible Subjects.* Syracuse, NY: Syracuse University Press, 2008.

Jason, Stephanie M. "Obstruction, Lies and Dishonor: Hillary's Benghazi Legacy." *The Hill*, July 5, 2016. https://thehill .com/blogs/pundits-blog/foreign-policy/286438-obstruction-lies-and-dishonor-hillarys-benghazi-legacy.

Jefferson, Thomas. "Extract from Thomas Jefferson to Edward Carrington." *The Jefferson Monticello*, January 16, 1787. https://tjrs.monticello.org/letter/1289.

Jenness, Valerie. "Explaining Criminalization: From Demography and Status Politics to Globalization and Modernization." *Annual Review of Sociology* 30 (2004): 147–171.

John Hagee Ministries/Facebook, "Megachurch Pastor John Hagee is Not the 'Discoverer' of the Pattern of Blood Moons, According to News Reports from 'WND.'" In Jennifer LeClaire, "John Hagee's Ministry Responds to 'Four Blood Moons' Allegations," March 23, 2015. https://www.charismanews.com/us/48861-john-hagee-responds-to -allegations-he-stole-four-blood-moons-revelation.

Johnson, Jenna, and Abigail Hauslohner. "'I Think Islam Hates Us': A Timeline of Trump's Comments about Islam and Muslims." *Washington Post*, May 20, 2017. https://www.washingtonpost.com/news/post-politics/wp/2017/05/20/i -think-islam-hates-us-a-timeline-of-trumps-comments-about-islam-and-muslims/.

Jones, Robert P., Daniel Cox, William A. Galston, and E.J. Dionne, Jr. "What It Means to Be an American: Attitudes in an Increasingly Diverse America Ten Years after 9/11." *Brookings and Public Religion Research Institute*, September 6, 2011. https://www.brookings.edu/research/what-it-means to -be-an-american-attitudes-in-an-increasingly-diverse -america-ten-years-after-911/.

Kaplan, Rebecca. "Hillary Clinton: U.S. Should Take 65,000 Syrian Refugees." *Face the Nation*, September 20, 2015. https://www.cbsnews.com/news/hillary-clinton-u-s-should-take-65000-syrian-refugees/.

Karson, Kendall. "Trump Says Players Who Don't Stand for Anthem 'Shouldn't Be in the Country.'" *ABC News*, May 24, 2018. https://abcnews.go.com/Politics/nfl-players-stand-national-anthem-shouldnt-country-trump/story?id= 55403960.

Kaufman, Moisés and the members of the Tectonic Theatre Project. *The Laramie Project and The Laramie Project: Ten Years Later*. New York, NY: Vintage, 2014.

Kaufman, Sarah Beth. "The Criminalization of Muslims in the US, 2016." *Qualitative Sociology* 42, no. 4 (2019): 521–542.

Kaufman, Sarah Beth, and Hanna Niner. "Muslim Victimization in the Contemporary US: Clarifying the Racialization Thesis." *Critical Criminology* 27 (2019): 485–502.

Kawai, Yuko. "Stereotyping Asian Americans: The Dialectic of the Model Minority and the Yellow Peril." *Howard Journal of Communication* 16, no. 2 (2005): 109–130.

Khan, Saeed A. "Sharia Law, Islamophobia and the US Constitution: New Tectonic Plates of the Culture Wars." *University of Maryland Law Journal of Race, Religion, Gender and Class* 12, no. 1 (2012): 123.

Kruzel, John. "Donald Trump Is Wrong About the Pulse Nightclub Shooting." *Politifact*, March 1, 2018. http:// www.politifact.com/truth-o-meter/statements/2018/mar/01/donald-trump/donald-trump-wrong-about -pulse-nightclub-shooting/.

Kundnani, Arun. *The Muslims Are Coming!: Islamophobia, Extremism, and the Domestic War on Terror*. London: Verso Trade, 2014.

Lane, David. *Contemporary British Drama*. Edinburgh: Edinburgh University Press, 2010.

Lean, Nathan. *The Islamophobia Industry: How the Right Manufactures Hatred of Muslims*. London: Pluto Press, 2017.

Levin, Brian. "Hate Crime Analysis and Forecast for 2016/2017." *Center for the Study of Hate Crime and Extremism*. (2018) Available at https://csbs.csusb.edu/sites/csusb_csbs/files/Final%20Hate%20Crime%2017%20Status%20 Report%20pdf.pdf.

Levinson, Matt. "Transdisciplinarity: Thinking Inside and Outside the Box." *Edutopia*, January 21, 2016. https://www .edutopia.org/blog/transdiciplinarity-thinking-inside-outside-box-matt-levinson.

Lipka, Michael. "Muslims and Islam: Key Findings in the U.S. and Around the World." Pew Research Center. August 9, 2017. http://www.pewresearch.org/fact-tank/2017/08/09/muslims-and-islam-key-findings-in-the-u-s-and-around -the-world/.

Locher, John (AP). "President-Elect Donald Trump Gives His Acceptance Speech During His Election Night Rally, Wednesday, Nov. 9, 2016, in New York." *Las Vegas Review Journal*, November 9, 2016. https://www.reviewjournal .com/news/politics-and-government/donald-trump-wins-2016-presidential-election/.

Mamdani, Mahmood. *Good Muslim, Bad Muslim: America, the Cold War, and the Roots of Terror*. New York: Three Leaves Press/Pantheon, 2005.

Mantyla, Kyle. "John Hagee: God Will Hold You Accountable for Not Voting for Donald Trump." *Right Wing Watch*, May 18, 2016. https://www.rightwingwatch.org/post/john-hagee-god-will-hold-you-accountable-for-not-voting -for-donald-trump/.

Marable, Manning. *Malcolm X: A Life of Reinvention*. New York: Penguin, 2011.

Marranci, Gabriele. "Multiculturalism, Islam and the Clash of Civilisations Theory: Rethinking Islamophobia." *Culture and Religion* 5, no. 1 (2004): 105–117.

Marzouki, Nadia. *Islam: An American Religion*. New York: Columbia University Press, 2017.

McCombs, Maxwell. "The Agenda Setting Approach." In *Handbook of Political Communication*, edited by Dan D. Nimmo and Keith R. Sanders, 121–140. Beverly Hills: Sage Publications, 1981.

McCombs, Maxwell. "Explorers and Surveyors: Expanding Strategies for Agenda Setting Research." *Journalism Quarterly* 69 (1992): 813–824.

McCombs, Maxwell. *Setting the Agenda: Mass Media and Public Opinion* (second edition). Malden, MA: Polity Press, 2018.

McCombs, Maxwell, and Donald L. Shaw. "The Agenda-Setting Function of Mass Media." *Public Opinion Quarterly* 36, no. 2 (1972): 176–187.

Mohamed, Besheer. "A New Estimate of the U.S. Muslim Population." *Pew Research Center*. January 6, 2016. Available at https://www.pewresearch.org/fact-tank/2016/01/06/a-new-estimate-of-the-u-s-muslim-population/.

Mondon, Aurelien, and Aaron Winter. "Articulations of Islamophobia: From the Extreme to the Mainstream?" *Ethnic and Racial Studies* 40, no. 13 (2017): 2151–2179.

Morgan, George, and Scott Poynting, eds. *Global Islamophobia: Muslims and Moral Panic in the West*. New York, NY: Routledge, 2012.

MSNBC. "Donald Trump: If I Win, Syrian Refugees 'Are Going Back,'" *MSNBC*, September 30, 2015. https://www.youtube.com/watch?v=cy4QZ5gdkyg.

Muslim Arbitrational Tribunal. "History." Accessed November 29, 2019. http://www.matribunal.com/history.php.

New York Times. "National Exit Polls: How Different Groups Voted." https://www.nytimes.com/interactive/2020/11/03/us/elections/exit-polls-president.html.

Ngan, Mandel (AF/Getty Images). In Jen Wieczner, "The Stock Market Just Voted for Hillary Clinton for President." *Fortune*, November 7, 2016. https://fortune.com/2016/11/07/trump-hillary-clinton-election-gold-peso-stocks/.

Norton, Anne. *On the Muslim Question*. Princeton, NJ: Princeton University Press, 2013.

O'Brien, Peter. *The Muslim Question in Europe*. Philadelphia: Temple University Press, 2016.

O'Hare, William P. "What Data from the 2010 Census Tell Us about the Changing Child Population of the United States." *Population Research and Policy Review* 32 (2013): 767–789. https://doi.org/10.1007/s11113-013-9267-8.

Omi, Michael, and Howard Winant. *Racial Formation in the United States: From the 1960s to the 1990s*, Second Edition. New York City: Routledge, 1994.

Parvini, Sarah, and Ellis Simani. "Are Arabs and Iranians White? Census Says Yes, but Many Disagree." *Los Angeles Times*, March 28, 2019. https://www.latimes.com/projects/la-me-census-middle-east-north-africa-race/.

Pew Research Center. "U.S. Muslims Concerned About Their Place in Society, but Continue to Believe in the American Dream." July 26, 2017. https://www.pewforum.org/2017/07/26/findings-from-pew-research-centers-2017-survey-of-us-muslims/.

Piscator, Erwin. *The Political Theatre*. Translated by Hugh Rorrison. London: Methuen, 1980.

Popper, Karl. *The Open Society and Its Enemies*. Princeton: Princeton University Press, 2013.

PRRI/Brookings. "PRRI/Brookings 2016 Immigration Survey." June 23, 2016. https://www.prri.org/wp-content/uploads/2017/12/PRRI-Brookings-2016-Immigration-Survey-Topline-FINAL.pdf.

Quinn, Ben. "French Police Make Woman Remove Clothing on Nice Beach Following Burkini Ban." *The Guardian*, August 23, 2016. https://www.theguardian.com/world/2016/aug/24/french-police-make-woman-remove-burkini-on-nice-beach#:~:text=Authorities%20in%20several%20French%20towns,terrorist%20killings%20in%20the%20country.

Quraishi-Landes, Asifa. "Legal Pluralism in an Islamic State: Reflections on the Afghan Constitution." *HBORL Working Paper No. 2015/02*. Edited by Tilmann J. Röder and Sayed Hameed Zia, (Hamida Barmaki Organization for the Rule of Law, 2015). http://www.hborl.org.af/wp-content/uploads/2017/09/HBORL-WP-2015-02-Quraishi_Legal -Pluralism.pdf.

Quraishi-Landes, Asifa. "Rumors of the Sharia Threat Are Greatly Exaggerated: What American Judges Really Do with Islamic Family Law in Their Courtrooms." *NYLS Law Review* 57, no. 2 (2013): 245–257.

Rana, Junaid. *Terrifying Muslims: Race and Labor in the South Asian Diaspora*. Durham, NC: Duke University Press, 2011.

Razack, Sherene. *Casting Out: The Eviction of Muslims from Western Law and Politics*. Toronto, Canada: University of Toronto Press, 2008.

Reuters. "The Immediate Aftermath of a Coalition Airstrike on Syria in October, 2015." In Paul Wood and Richard Hall, "The US is Killing More Civilians in Iraq and Syria than it Acknowledges." *The World*, February 1, 2016. https://www .pri.org/stories/2016-02-01/us-killing-more-civilians-iraq-and-syria-it-acknowledges.

Russo, Ann. "The Feminist Majority Foundation's Campaign to Stop Gender Apartheid: The Intersections of Feminism and Imperialism in the United States." *International Feminist Journal of Politics* 8, no. 4 (2006): 557–580.

Said, Edward W. *Covering Islam: How the Media and the Experts Determine How We See the Rest of the World (Fully revised edition)*. New York: Random House, 2008.

Said, Omar Ibn. *A Muslim American Slave: The Life of Omar Ibn Said*. Translated by Ala Alryyes. Madison: University of Wisconsin Press, 2011.

Santucci, John. "Donald Trump Insists Muslim Ban Is About Safety, Not Religion." *ABC*, December 9, 2015. http:// abcnews.go.com/Politics/donald-trump-insists-muslim ban-safety-religion/story?id=35666498.

Scheufele, Dietram A. "Agenda-Setting, Priming, and Framing Revisited: Another Look at Cognitive Effects of Political Communication," *Mass Communication & Society* 3 (2000): 297–316.

Scheufele, Dietram A., and David Tewksbury. "Framing, Agenda Setting, and Priming: The Evolution of Three Media Effects Models," *Journal of Communication* 57, no. 1 (2007): 9–20.

Schwartz, Ian. "Sen. Graham: 'Trump Understands We Are in A Religious War.'" *Real Clear Politics*, November 1, 2017. https://www.realclearpolitics.com/video/2017/11/01/sen_graham_trump_understand_we_are_in_a_religious _war.html#!.

Sedorowitz, Marion. "Oral History Interview Conducted by Liz H. Strong." Muslims in Brooklyn oral histories, *Brooklyn Historical Society*, April 11, 2018. https://oralhistory.brooklynhistory.org/interviews/sedorowitz-marion -20180411/.

Selod, Saher. "Citizenship Denied: The Racialization of Muslim American Men and Women Post-9/11." *Critical Sociology* 41, no. 1 (2015): 77–95.

Selod, Saher. *Forever Suspect: Racialized Surveillance of Muslims in the War on Terror*. New Brunswick, NJ: Rutgers University Press, 2018.

Sewell, William H. "Historical Events as Transformations of Structures: Inventing Revolution at the Bastille." *Theory and Society* 25, no. 6 (1996): 841–881.

Shafer, Jack. "16 Stories That Changed the 2016 Race." *Politico*, November 6, 2016. https://www.politico.com/story /2016/11/2016-election-biggest-stories-230790.

Shaheen, Jack G. *Reel Bad Arabs: How Hollywood Vilifies a People*. Northampton, MA: Interlink Publishing, 2012.

Shoemaker, Pamela J., and Stephen D. Reese. *Mediating the Message* (2nd ed.). White Plains, NY: Longman, 1996.

Silliman, Jael, and Annanya Bhattacharjee. *Policing the National Body: Race, Gender, and Criminalization*. Cambridge, MA: South End Press, 2002.

Smith, David. "Where Donald Trump and Hillary Clinton Stand on 2016's Key Issues." *The Guardian*, June 9, 2016. https:// www.theguardian.com/us-news/2016/jun/09/trump-clinton-economy-immigration-gun-control-environment.

Smith, Gregory. "Most White Evangelicals Approve of Trump Travel Prohibition and Express Concerns about Extremism." *Pew Research Center*, February 27, 2017. http://www.pewresearch.org/fact-tank/2017/02/27/most-white -evangelicals-approve-of-trump-travel-prohibition-and-express-concerns-about-extremism/.

Spellberg, Denise A. *Thomas Jefferson's Qur'an: Islam and the Founders*. New York: Vintage, 2013.

Trump, Donald J. "Donald J. Trump Statement on Preventing Muslim Immigration." Press Release. Donald J. Trump Presidential Campaign, December 7, 2015. https://www.presidency.ucsb.edu/documents/statement-donald-j-trump -statement-preventing-muslim-immigration.

Trump, Donald J. "Protecting the Nation from Foreign Terrorist Entry into the United States." *Federal Register*, March 7, 2017. https://www.federalregister.gov/documents/2017/03/09/2017-04837/protecting-the-nation-from-foreign -terrorist-entry-into-the-united-states.

Trump, Donald, J. "Suspension of Entry as Immigrants and Nonimmigrants of Certain Additional Persons Who Pose a Risk of Transmitting 2019 Novel Coronavirus." *The White House*, January 25, 2021. https://www.whitehouse.gov /briefing-room/presidential-actions/2021/01/25/proclamation-on-the-suspension-of-entry-as-immigrants-and -non-immigrants-of-certain-additional-persons-who-pose-a-risk-of-transmitting-coronavirus-disease/.

Weiss, Peter. *The Investigation: A Play*. Translated by Jon Swan and Ulu Grosbard. New York: Atheneum, 1966.

Williams, Raymond. 1977. *Marxism and Literature*. Oxford: Oxford University Press.

Wuthnow, Robert. *America and the Challenges of Religious Diversity*. Princeton, NJ: Princeton University Press, 2007.

Yukich, Grace, and Penny Edgell, eds. *Religion as Raced: Understanding American Religion in the Twenty-First Century*. New York, NY: New York University Press, 2020.

Zakaria, Fareed. "The Politics of Rage: Why Do They Hate Us?" *Newsweek* 138, no. 16 (2001): 22–25.

NOTES

INTRODUCTION

1. Moisés Kaufman and the members of the Tectonic Theater Project, *The Laramie Project and The Laramie Project: Ten Years Later* (New York, NY: Vintage, 2014): iv.

2. Though there was little discussion of Islam in the 2020 campaign, the Trump Administration used COVID-19 as a marker of difference in his drive to curb immigration. See Donald J. Trump, "Suspension of Entry as Immigrants and Nonimmigrants of Certain Additional Persons Who Pose a Risk of Transmitting 2019 Novel Corona-virus," White House, March 11, 2020, https://www.whitehouse.gov/briefing-room/presidential-actions/2021/01/25/proclamation-on-the-suspension-of-entry-as-immigrants-and-non-immigrants-of-certain-additional-persons-who-pose-a-risk-of-transmitting-coronavirus-disease/.

3. See the transcript of his interview on ABC's "Live with Kelly and Michael." John Santucci, "Donald Trump Insists Muslim Ban Is About Safety, Not Religion," *ABC*, December 9, 2015, http://abcnews.go.com/Politics/donald-trump-insists-muslim ban-safety-religion/story?id=35666498.

4. Christopher Bail, *Terrified: How Anti-Muslim Fringe Organizations Became Mainstream* (Princeton, NJ: Princeton University Press, 2015).

5. Gregory Smith, "Most White Evangelicals Approve of Trump Travel Prohibition and Express Concerns about Extremism," *Pew Research Center*, February 27, 2017, http://www.pewresearch.org/fact-tank/2017/02/27/most-white-evangelicals-approve-of-trump-travel-prohibition-and-express-concerns-about-extremism/.

6. See George W. Bush's Whitehouse Archives, "Backgrounder: The President's Quotes on Islam." The White House. Accessed February 15, 2021, https://georgewbush-whitehouse.archives.gov/infocus/ramadan/islam.html.

7. Jenna Johnson and Abigail Hauslohner, "'I Think Islam Hates Us': A Timeline of Trump's Comments about Islam and Muslims," *Washington Post*, May 20, 2017, https://www.washingtonpost.com/news/post-politics/wp/2017/05/20/i-think-islam-hates-us-a-timeline-of-trumps-comments-about-islam-and-muslims/.

8. Sarah Parvini and Ellis Simani, "Are Arabs and Iranians White? Census Says Yes, but Many Disagree," *Los Angeles Times*, March 28, 2019, https://www.latimes.com/projects/la-me-census-middle-east-north-africa-race/. These racial cate-gories can be viewed as constructions of an imperial gaze rather than real, lived experiences, but nonetheless illustrate diversity among Muslim Americans.

9. See Michael Lipka, "Muslims and Islam: Key Findings in the U.S. and Around the World," *Pew Research Center*, August 9, 2017, http://www.pewresearch.org/fact-tank/2017/08/09/muslims-and-islam-key-findings-in-the-u-s-and-around-the-world/; and *Pew Research Center*, "U.S. Muslims Concerned About Their Place in Society, but Continue to Believe in the American Dream," July 26, 2017, http://assets.pewresearch.org/wp-content/uploads/sites/11/2017/07/09105631/U.S.-MUSLIMS-FULL-REPORT-with-population-update-v2.pdf.

10. ACLU, "Timeline of the Muslim Ban," accessed February 15, 2021, https://www.aclu-wa.org/pages/timeline-muslim-ban.

11. See the full text of this ban at Donald Trump, "Protecting the Nation from Foreign Terrorist Entry into the United States," Federal Registry, March 7, 2017, https://www.federalregister.gov/documents/2017/03/09/2017-04837/protecting-the-nation-from-foreign-terrorist-entry-into-the-united-states.

12. Todd Green, "By Any Other Name: Why the 'Travel Ban' Really is a Muslim Ban," July 3, 2018, https://religion news.com/2018/07/03/by-any-other-name-why-the-travel-ban-really-is-a-muslim-ban/.

13. See for example, William H. Sewell, Jr., "Historical Events as Transformations of Structures: Inventing Revolution at the Bastille," *Theory and Society* 25, no 6 (1996): 841–881.

14. Raymond Williams, *Marxism and Literature*, (Oxford: Oxford University Press, 1977).

15. An insight influenced by Courtney Abrams, Karen Albright, and Aaron Panofsky, "Contesting the New York Community: From Liminality to the 'New Normal' in the Wake of September 11," *City and Community* 3, 3 (2004): 189–220.

16. See for example, PPRI/Brooking's poll, available at: https://www.prri.org/wp-content/uploads/2017/12/PRRI -Brookings-2016-Immigration-Survey-Topline-FINAL.pdf (pg. 14, question 13F).

17. The full interview guide is reproduced in Appendix A. For a full description of the study's method, see Sarah Beth Kaufman, "The Criminalization of Muslims in the United States, 2016" *Qualitative Sociology* 42, no. 4 (2019): 521–542.

18. For an overview of this demographic shift, see William P. O'Hare, "What Data from the 2010 Census Tell Us about the Changing Child Population of the United States." *Population Research and Policy Review* 32 (2013): 767–789. https:// doi.org/10.1007/s11113-013-9267-8. According to the U.S. Census Bureau, San Antonio's residents are 64% are Latino, with the median household income well below the national average.

19. Bexar County Elections Department, "November 8, 2016 Election Totals Report," November 8, 2016, https:// www.bexar.org/DocumentCenter/View/9438/November-8-2016-Media-Report.

20. Derek Edwards and Alessandra Fasulo, "To Be Honest: Sequential Uses of Honesty Phrases in Talk-In-Interaction," *Research on Language and Social Interaction* 39, no. 4 (2006): 343–376.

21. It is worth noting that voters' concerns polled differently in 2016 and 2020. In 2020, voters' primary concerns were the economy, racial inequality, the coronavirus, crime and safety, and healthcare ["National Exit Polls: How Different Groups Voted," *New York Times*, https://www.nytimes.com/interactive/2020/11/03/us/elections/exit-polls-president.html].

22. Wajahat Ali, Eli Clifton, Matthew Duss, Lee Fang, Scott Keyes, and Faiz Shakir. "Fear, Inc. The Roots of the Islamophobia Network in America," *The Center for American Progress*, (August 26, 2016).

23. For a brief overview of this mischaracterization of sharia, see Asifa Quraishi-Landes, "Rumors of the Sharia Threat Are Greatly Exaggerated: What American Judges Really Do with Islamic Family Law in their Courtrooms," *New York Law School Law Review* 57 (2012): 245.

PART I   TO BE HONEST: VOICES ON DONALD TRUMP'S MUSLIM BAN

24. The videotaped segment that begins the play is from a speech given by Donald Trump: "Clip of Presidential Candidate Donald Trump Rally in Mount Pleasant, South Carolina," *C-SPAN*, December 7, 2015, https://www.c-span .org/video/?c4566084/user-clip-donald-trummp-ban-muslim [00:24–01:07].

25. Slide of Trump and Clinton: Mandel Ngan (AF)/Getty Images), in Jen Wieczner, "The Stock Market Just Voted for Hillary Clinton for President," *Fortune*, November 7, 2016, https://fortune.com/2016/11/07/trump-hillary -clinton-election-gold-peso-stocks/.

26. Slide of U.S. Senator Ted Cruz: https://www.c-span.org/video/?411887-1/hearing-examines-term-radical-islam -terrorism-fight; Audio clip of Ted Cruz: "Debate on 'Radical Islam' and Terrorism," *C-SPAN*, June 28, 2016, https:// www.c-span.org/video/?411887-1/hearing-examines-use-term-radical-islam-terrorism-fight [12:19–12:36].

27. Slide of Sikh person who was attacked: The Sikh Coalition, in Kristine Guerra, "Calif. Attackers Assault Sikh Man, Removed His Turban, Cut Off His Hair," *NDTV*, October 10, 2016, https://www.ndtv.com/indians-abroad /calif-attackers-assault-sikh-man-removed-his-turban-cut-off-his-hair-1472310.

28. Slide of airstrike in Syria: Reuters, "The Immediate Aftermath of a Coalition Airstrike on Syria in October, 2015," in Paul Wood and Richard Hall, "The US is Killing More Civilians in Iraq and Syria than it Acknowledges," *The World*, February 1, 2016, https://www.pri.org/stories/2016-02-01/us-killing-more-civilians-iraq-and-syria-it-acknowledges.

29. Slide of Pulse shooting aftermath: Carlo Allegri (Reuters), "Police Forensics Investigators Work on June 12 at the Scene of the Mass Shooting at the Pulse Nightclub in Orlando," in Adam Goldman and Mark Berman, "'They Took Too Damn Long': Inside the Police Response to the Orlando Shooting," *The Washington Post*, August 1, 2016, https://www.washingtonpost.com/world/national-security/they-took-too-damn-long-inside-the-police-response-to-the-orlando-shooting/2016/08/01/67a66130-5447-11e6-88eb-7dda4e2f2aec_story.html.

30. Slide of Muslims standing up to terrorists who say they act in the name of Islam: "#notinmyname: Fighting Extremism," *CNN*, September 18, 2014, https://www.cnn.com/2014/09/18/world/gallery/not-in-my-name/index.html.

31. Slide of John Hagee: John Hagee Ministries/Facebook, "Megachurch Pastor John Hagee is Not the 'Discoverer' of the Pattern of Blood Moons, According to News Reports from 'WND,'" in Jennifer LeClaire, "John Hagee's Ministry Responds to 'Four Blood Moons' Allegations," March 23, 2015, https://www.charismanews.com/us/48861-john-hagee-responds-to-allegations-he-stole-four-blood-moons-revelation; Audio clip of John Hagee: Kyle Mantyla, "John Hagee: God Will Hold You Accountable For Not Voting For Donald Trump," *Right Wing Watch*, May 18, 2016, https://www.rightwingwatch.org/post/john-hagee-god-will-hold-you-accountable-for-not-voting-for-donald-trump/ [00:20-00:27; 00:39-00:48; 00:50-00:54; 01:06-01:15].

32. Slide of Bernie Sanders giving tribute: Getty Images. "Bernie Sanders described himself as a 'bit of a boxing' fan as he paid tribute to Muhammad Ali," in Robert Costa, "Bernie Sanders pays tribute to Muhammad Ali for 'courageous' opposition to Vietnam War," *Independent*, June 5, 2016, https://www.independent.co.uk/news/people/muhammad-ali-dead-bernie-sanders-tribute-vietnam-war-us-election-a7066296.html; Audio clip of Bernie Sanders: "Sanders pays tribute to Muhammad Ali," Channel 4 News, June 5, 2016, https://www.facebook.com/watch/?v=10153796081356939 [00:00-00:25].

33. Slide of women in burkinis: AFP Getty, "A Woman in a Burkini, a Woman in a Bikini and a Woman in a Swimming Costume on a Beach Near Bizerte," in Romina McGuinness and Alice Foster, "What is the Burkini? Why Have French Towns Banned the Full-Body Swimsuit?" *Express*, August 18, 2016, https://www.express.co.uk/news/world/701626/Burkini-what-is-full-body-swimsuit-Muslim-swimmers-French-ban-towns-France-fine-burka.

34. Slide of grieving men after cleric and his associate are killed: Stephanie Keith (Reuters), "A Crowd of Community Members Gather at the Place Where Imam Maulama Akonjee was Killed in the Queens Borough of New York City, August 13, 2016," in *Fortune*, August 14, 2016, "Muslim Cleric and Associate Shot to Death on New York Street," http://fortune.com/2016/08/14/muslim-cleric-shot-to-death-nyc/.

35. Slide of ISIS attack on Baghdad shopping center: AP, "Iraqi Security Forces and Civilians Gather at the Site After a Car Bomb Hit Karada, a Busy Shopping District in the Center of Baghdad, Iraq," in Lizzie Dearden, "Baghdad Attack: Death Toll from Isis Bombing Rises to 250 in Deadliest Explosion to Hit Iraq Capital Since 2003," *Independent*, July 6, 2016, https://www.independent.co.uk/news/world/middle-east/baghdad-bombing-attack-latest-news-isis-islamic-state-death-toll-shopping-centre-ramadan-shia-a7122196.html.

36. Slide of soldier holding drowned child: Nilufer Demir (AFP/Getty Images), "A Turkish Paramilitary Police Officer Carries the Body of 2-year-old Syrian Refugee Alan Kurdi, Found Washed Ashore Near the Turkish Resort of Bodrum in September 2015," in Diane Cole, "Following Up: The Aunt Of The Drowned Syrian Boy Tells What Happened After The Tragedy," *National Public Radio*, August 31, 2018, https://www.npr.org/sections/goatsandsoda/2018/08/31/642952840/an-aunts-memoir-remembering-the-drowned-syrian-boy-on-the-beach; Audio clips of Clinton and Trump: Clinton audio: Rebecca Kaplan, "Hillary Clinton: U.S. Should Take 65,000 Syrian Refugees," *Face the Nation*, September 20, 2015, https://www.cbsnews.com/news/hillary-clinton-u-s-should-take-65000-syrian-refugees/ [00:19-00:22]; Trump audio: "Donald Trump: If I Win, Syrian Refugees 'Are Going Back,'" MSNBC, September 30, 2015, https://www.youtube.com/watch?v=cy4QZ5gdkyg [00:36-00:47].

37. Slide of President-Elect Trump: John Locher (AP), "President-Elect Donald Trump Gives His Acceptance Speech During His Election Night Rally, Wednesday, Nov. 9, 2016, in New York," *Las Vegas Review Journal*, November 9, 2016, https://www.reviewjournal.com/news/politics-and-government/donald-trump-wins-2016-presidential-election/.

PART II   UNDERSTANDING *TO BE HONEST*

38. Augusto Boal, *Theater of the Oppressed* (New York: Theater Communications Group, 1985), 122.

39. Matt Levinson, "Transdisciplinarity: Thinking Inside and Outside the Box," *Edutopia*, January 21, 2016, https://www.edutopia.org/blog/transdiciplinarity-thinking-inside-outside-box-matt-levinson.

40. Samuel Taylor Coleridge, *Biographia Literaria*, ed. Adam Roberts (Edinburgh: Edinburgh University Press, 2014), 208.

41. Jürgen Habermas, *The Structural Transformation of the Public Sphere: An Inquiry into a Category of Bourgeois Society*, trans. Thomas Burger (Cambridge: MIT Press, 1989), 36–37.

42. Habermas, *The Structural Transformation of the Public Sphere*, 33–34.

43. Habermas, *The Structural Transformation of the Public Sphere*, 36–37.

44. Erwin Piscator, *The Political Theater*, trans. Hugh Rorrison (London: Methuen, 1980).

45. Hallie Flanagan, *Arena: The History of the Federal Theater* (New York: Benjamin Blom, 1940), 16.

46. Bertolt Brecht, *Brecht on Theater*, trans. John Willett (New York: Hill and Wang, 1964), 43.

47. Brecht, *Brecht on Theater*, 44.

48. Peter Weiss, *The Investigation: A Play*, trans. Jon Swan and Ulu Grosbard (New York: Atheneum, 1966).

49. Eric Bentley, *Are You Now or Have You Ever Been?* (New York: Samuel French, 1979).

50. Frank Condon and Ron Sossi, *The Chicago Conspiracy Trial: A Theatrical Arrangement of the Original Trial Transcripts* (New York: Theater Communications Group, 1979).

51. David Lane, *Contemporary British Drama* (Edinburgh: Edinburgh University Press, 2010), 65.

52. Lane, *Contemporary British Drama*, 65.

53. Thomas Jefferson, "Extract from Thomas Jefferson to Edward Carrington," *The Jefferson Monticello*, January 16, 1787, https://tjrs.monticello.org/letter/1289.

54. See Jack Shafer, "16 Stories That Changed the 2016 Race," *Politico*, November 6, 2016, https://www.politico.com/story/2016/11/2016-election-biggest-stories-230790.

For a timeline of the presidential campaign see Lauren Gambino and Madhvi Pankhania, "How We Got Here: A Complete Timeline of 2016's Historic US Election," *The Guardian*, November 8, 2016, https://www.theguardian.com/us-news/2016/nov/07/us-election-2016-complete-timeline-clinton-trump-president.

55. For a story on where the candidates stood on key issues, see David Smith, "Where Donald Trump and Hillary Clinton Stand on 2016's Key Issues," *The Guardian*, June 9, 2016, https://www.theguardian.com/us-news/2016/jun/09/trump-clinton-economy-immigration-gun-control-environment. Also, the rise of social media has provided platforms where politicians can bypass, attack, or support legacy news organizations.

56. Stephanie M. Jason, "Obstruction, Lies and Dishonor: Hillary's Benghazi Legacy," *The Hill*, July 5, 2016, https://thehill.com/blogs/pundits-blog/foreign-policy/286438-obstruction-lies-and-dishonor-hillarys-benghazi-legacy.

57. Kendall Karson, "Trump Says Players Who Don't Stand for Anthem 'Shouldn't Be in the Country,'" *ABC News*, May 24, 2018, https://abcnews.go.com/Politics/nfl-players-stand-national-anthem-shouldnt-country-trump/story?id=55403960.

58. Though there is disagreement about the definitional and theoretical underpinnings of agenda-setting, framing, and priming [see Dietram A. Scheufele, "Agenda-Setting, Priming, and Framing Revisited: Another Look at Cognitive Effects of Political Communication," *Mass Communication & Society 3* (2000): 297–316 and Dietram A. Scheufele and David

Tewksbury, "Framing, Agenda Setting, and Priming: The Evolution of Three Media Effects Models," *Journal of Communication* 57, no. 1 (2007): 9–20.], there is agreement that the news can do all three things.

59. From a theatrical viewpoint, news stories provide a dramatic transition between episodes that allow the actors to get on and off the stage and, at times, to "interact" with what is being shown on the screen. For example, at the beginning and end of the play, the script indicates that all the actors are on stage and they should all be looking at the "television" screen. The idea is that no matter who you are or what opinions you hold, you must deal with Donald Trump's Islamic world view and his presidency.

60. See Maxwell McCombs, "The Agenda Setting Approach," in *Handbook of Political Communication*, (Beverly Hills, CA: Sage, 1981), 121–140; Maxwell McCombs, "Explorers and Surveyors: Expanding Strategies for Agenda Setting Research," *Journalism Quarterly* 69 (1992): 813–824; Maxwell McCombs, *Setting the Agenda: Mass Media and Public Opinion* (2nd edition) (Malden, MA: Polity Press, 2018); Maxwell McCombs and Donald L. Shaw, "The Agenda-Setting Function of Mass Media," *Public Opinion Quarterly* 36, no. 2 (1972): 176–187.

61. With the rise of cable and the Internet and more opportunities for people, the idea that only white men should read the news is now considered antiquated. So, what voice or voices should be used in the play? Originally, each of the news clips was read by the "interviewer" as a way of providing continuity throughout the piece. After workshopping the performance, it was decided to use a professional newsperson to read the news stories. After additional workshopping, it was decided that different voices needed to be heard along with the use of actual audio clips, where available. Currently, the play uses voice "actualities" [actualities are where the actual voices of the people are heard] of Ted Cruz, John Hagee, Bernie Sanders, Hillary Clinton, and Donald Trump.

62. We used Senator Cruz's voice.

63. We used a second female voice.

64. Candidate Trump made the case that if someone in the club had been armed, the carnage would not have happened. See: John Kruzel, "Donald Trump Is Wrong About the Pulse Nightclub Shooting," *Politifact*, March 1, 2018, http://www .politifact.com/truth-o-meter/statements/2018/mar/01/donald-trump/donald-trump-wrong-about-pulse-nightclub -shooting/.

65. The agenda-setting function of some of the news clips in the play was to help advance the narrative by telling people what to think about. Of course, many of the news stories that were reported would have been known to the audience and they would have interpreted them through their own frames.

66. Framing is seen as both a macro- and micro-construct. "As a macroconstruct, the term 'framing' refers to modes of presentation that journalists and communicators use to present information in a way that resonates with existing underlying schemas among their audience (Shoemaker and Reese 1996)." "As a microconstruct, framing describes how people use information and presentation features regarding issues as they form impressions." Dietram A. Scheufele and David Tewksbury, "Framing, Agenda Setting, and Priming: The Evolution of Three Media Effects Model": 12.

67. Scheufele and Tewksbury, 11.

68. Priming suggests what specific issues people "ought to use . . . as benchmarks for evaluating the performance of leaders and governments." Said another way, "By making some issues more salient in people's minds (agenda setting), mass media can also shape the considerations that people take into account when making judgments about political candidates or issues (priming)." Dietram A. Scheufele and David Tewksbury, 11.

69. We used a second, male professional radio voice for this episode.

70. Asifa Quraishi-Landes, "Legal Pluralism in an Islamic State: Reflections on the Afghan Constitution." *HBORL Working Paper No. 2015/02*, eds. Tilmann J. Röder and Sayed Hameed Zia, (Hamida Barmaki Organization for the Rule of Law. 2015): 10, http://www.hborl.org.af/wp-content/uploads/2017/09/HBORL-WP-2015-02-Quraishi_Legal -Pluralism.pdf.

71. In this episode we used the voice of a Muslim woman.

72. The audio used was Pastor Hagee's voice.

73. We hear Bernie Sanders's voice.

74. We had a native French speaker read the news about the burkini.

75. Ben Quinn, "French Police Make Woman Remove Clothing on Nice Beach Following Burkini Ban," *The Guardian*, August 23, 2016, https://www.theguardian.com/world/2016/aug/24/french-police-make-woman-remove-burkini-on -nice-beach#:~:text=Authorities%20in%20several%20French%20towns,terrorist%20killings%20in%20the%20country.

76. In one of the more poignant moments in the news clips, we used a young girl's voice to read the news to the audience.

77. There were five questions about specific news events that were asked during the interview process. These questions led to a discussion of older news stories: 1) Does this discussion around Islam remind you of any other political conversation in history? 2) Do you remember hearing about this story: A few weeks ago, young man had boarded a plane on Southwest Airlines when he was overheard speaking Arabic on the phone. A passenger alerted a crew member, and the young man was escorted off the plane and not allowed to fly. It was later confirmed that he was a U.S. citizen with no links to any terrorist organization. How would you feel if you witnessed this? 3) And do you remember this? A young couple, one American-born and the other Pakistan-born, shoot up a room full of people in San Bernardino, California, killing 14 and injuring 28 others. The FBI calls them "homegrown terrorists," "motivated by sympathy with extremist Islamic groups." They were not shown to have any official ties to terrorist groups. Do you think this is different from other mass shootings in the U.S.? 4) There is an argument that the police in the United States should be able to "stop and frisk" people they find suspicious. What do you think of this policy and would you support a similar policy for Muslims? 5) And, finally, can you remember how old you were when you first heard about Islam talked about in politics?

78. In order to encourage the audiences' processing of the play, we incorporated a talkback session after each performance. In some cases, the talkback session included the setting up of tables, where refreshments were available, and people were encouraged to sit and talk with their "neighbors" about what they had just experienced. In other cases, the talkback session was a question-and-answer session where audience members could ask the authors and actors questions. Some of the audience members commented that this post-performance session was the most valuable part of the production.

79. Anne Norton, *On the Muslim Question* (Princeton: Princeton University Press, 2013).

80. Samuel P. Huntington, "The Clash of Civilizations?" In *Culture and Politics: A Reader*, ed. Lane Crothers and Charles Lockhart (New York: Palgrave Macmillan, 2000), 99–118.

81. See Edward Said, *Covering Islam: How the Media and the Experts Determine How We See the Rest of the World (Fully revised edition)* (New York: Random House, 2008); Gabriele Marranci, "Multiculturalism, Islam and the Clash of Civilisations Theory: Rethinking Islamophobia," *Culture and Religion* 5, no. 1 (2004): 105–117.; Richard W. Bulliet, *The Case for Islamo-Christian Civilization* (New York: Columbia University Press, 2006); Todd H. Green, *The Fear of Islam: An Introduction to Islamophobia in the West* (Minneapolis: Augsburg Fortress Publishers, 2015).

82. Bulliet, *The Case for Islamo-Christian Civilization*.

83. Peter O'Brien, *The Muslim Question in Europe* (Philadelphia: Temple University Press, 2016).

84. Denise A Spellberg, *Thomas Jefferson's Qur'an: Islam and the Founders* (New York: Vintage, 2013), 75.

85. Spellberg, *Thomas Jefferson's Qur'an*; see also Omar Ibn Said, *A Muslim American Slave: The Life of Omar Ibn Said* (Madison: University of Wisconsin Press, 2011).

86. Nationality Act of 1940, as cited by Moustafa Bayoumi, "Racing Religion," *CR: The New Centennial Review* 6, no. 2 (2006): 267–293.

87. A year and a half later, a different judge accepted Hassan's admission to the United States because at that time Arabs could be considered "white." Bayoumi, "Racing Religion."

88. See Marion Sedorowitz, "Oral History Interview Conducted by Liz H. Strong," April 11, 2018, *Brooklyn Historical Society*, https://oralhistory.brooklynhistory.org/interviews/sedorowitz-marion-20180411/.

89. Manning Marable, *Malcolm X: A Life of Reinvention* (New York: Penguin, 2011).

90. Said, *Covering Islam*.

91. See the work of Jack Shaheen, *Reel Bad Arabs: How Hollywood Vilifies a People* (Northampton, MA: Interlink Publishing, 2012).

92. Fareed Zakaria, "The Politics of Rage: Why Do They Hate Us?" *Newsweek* 138, no. 16 (October 14, 2001): 22–25.

93. See study by Pew Research Center, "U.S. Muslims Concerned About Their Place in Society, but Continue to Believe in the American Dream," July 26, 2017, https://www.pewforum.org/2017/07/26/findings-from-pew-research-centers-2017-survey-of-us-muslims/.

94. Mahmood Mamdani, *Good Muslim, Bad Muslim: America, the Cold War, and the Roots of Terror.* (New York: Three Leaves Press/Pantheon, 2005).

95. See Wajahat Ali, Eli Clifton, Matthew Duss, Lee Fang, Scott Keyes, and Faiz Shakir.

"'Fear, Inc.': The Roots of the Islamophobia Network in America." Washington DC: *Center for American Progress,* August 26, 2011, https://www.americanprogress.org/issues/religion/reports/2011/08/26/10165/fear-inc/; Christopher Bail, *Terrified: How Anti-Muslim Fringe Organizations Became Mainstream.* (Princeton: Princeton University Press, 2014); Nathan Lean. *The Islamophobia Industry.* (London: Pluto Press, 2017).

96. Nadia Marzouki, *Islam: An American Religion* (New York: Columbia University Press, 2017).

97. Lean, *The Islamophobia Industry.*

98. Ali et al., *Fear, Inc.*

99. Bail, *Terrified.*

100. See Joel Gunter, "Trump's 'Muslim Lockdown': What is the Center for Security Policy?" *BBC News*, December 8, 2015, https://www.bbc.com/news/world-us-canada-35037943.

101. See https://www.splcenter.org/fighting-hate/extremist-files/group/center-security-policy.

102. Lauren Carroll and Louis Jacobson, "Trump Cites Shaky Survey in Call to Ban Muslims from Entering US," *Politifact*, December 9, 2015, https://www.politifact.com/factchecks/2015/dec/09/donald-trump/trump-cites-shaky-survey-call-ban-muslims-entering/.

103. Roland Barthes, *Image-Music-Text*, trans. Stephen Heath (New York: Macmillan, 1977).

104. Norman Fairclough, "Critical Discourse Analysis," in *How to Analyse Talk in Institutional Settings: A Casebook of Methods*, ed. A. McHoul and M. Rapley (London: Continuum, 2001), 25–38.

105. For a full transcript of the town hall, see CNN, "Transcript: CNN Presidential Town Hall: America's Military and The Commander and Chief," *CNN Press Room*, September 28, 2016. http://cnnpressroom.blogs.cnn.com/2016/09/28/transcript-cnn-presidential-town-hall-americas-military-and-the-commander-and-chief/.

106. https://www.cruz.senate.gov/?p=news&id=2987.

107. Examples of this include special registration for foreign Muslims which began in 2001, the Patriot Act which ushered in an era for domestic surveillance, and extra policing of Muslims in the New York area. See Sabrina Alimahomed-Wilson, "When the FBI Knocks: Racialized State Surveillance of Muslims." *Critical Sociology* 45, no. 6 (2019): 871–887.

108. Arun Kundnani, *The Muslims Are Coming!: Islamophobia, Extremism, and the Domestic War on Terror.* (London: Verso Trade, 2014).

109. Lean, *The Islamophobia Industry.*

110. Asifa Quraishi-Landes. "Rumors of the Sharia Threat Are Greatly Exaggerated: What American Judges Really Do with Islamic Family Law in Their Courtrooms." *NYL Sch. L. Rev.* 57 (2012): 245.

111. Leila Ahmed, *Women and Gender in Islam: Historical Roots of a Modern Debate* (New Haven, Yale University Press, 1992).

112. Ann Russo, "The Feminist Majority Foundation's Campaign to Stop Gender Apartheid: The Intersections of Feminism and Imperialism in the United States." *International Feminist Journal of Politics* 8, no. 4 (2006): 557–580.

113. Saher Selod, "Citizenship Denied: The Racialization of Muslim American Men and Women Post-9/11." *Critical Sociology* 41, no. 1 (2015): 77–95.

114. Ian Schwartz, "Sen. Graham: 'Trump Understands We Are in A Religious War,'" November 1, 2017, https://www.realclearpolitics.com/video/2017/11/01/sen_graham_trump_understand_we_are_in_a_religious_war.html#!.

115. Robert Wuthnow, *America and the Challenges of Religious Diversity* (Princeton, NJ: Princeton University Press, 2007), 163.

116.   Christopher Bail, *Terrified: How Anti-Muslim Fringe Organizations Became Mainstream* (Princeton, NJ: Princeton University Press, 2015), 111.

117.   Ruth Braunstein, "Muslims as Outsiders, Enemies, and Others: The 2016 Presidential Election and the Politics of Religious Exclusion," *American Journal of Cultural Sociology* 5, no. 3 (2017): 362–363.

118.   Muslim Arbitrational Tribunal, "History," accessed November 29, 2019, http://www.matribunal.com/history.php. One example of a sharia court in a Muslim-minority country is the English Muslim Arbitration Tribunal (MAT). The MAT's stated goal is to help English Muslims "[adhere] to the English Legal System whilst still preserving their personal practices of Islamic Sacred Law."

119.   Kambiz GhaneaBassiri, "Islamophobia and American History: Religious Stereotyping and Out-Grouping of Muslims in the United States," in *Islamophobia in America: The Anatomy of Intolerance*, ed. Carl W. Ernst (New York: Palgrave MacMillan, 2013), 58.

120.   Pipes is an American political scientist and professor known for speaking against "radical Islam" and in favor of "moderate Islam." Jay read this book in the early nineties, so he may have been referring to Pipes' book *In the Path of God: Islam and Political Power*, originally published in 1983.

121.   Richard Cimino, "'No God in Common:' American Evangelical Discourse on Islam after 9/11," *Review of Religious Research* 47, no. 2 (2005): 167.

122.   Amit A. Bhatia, "American Evangelicals and Islam: Their Perspectives, Attitudes and Practices Towards Muslims in the US," *Transformation: An International Journal of Holistic Mission Studies* 34, no. 1 (2017): 29.

123.   Robert P. Jones, Daniel Cox, William A. Galston, and E.J. Dionne, Jr., "What It Means to Be an American: Attitudes in an Increasingly Diverse America Ten Years after 9/11," Brookings and Public Religion Research Institute, September 6, 2011, https://www.brookings.edu/research/what-it-means-to-be-an-american-attitudes-in-an-increasingly-diverse-america-ten-years-after-911/.

124.   Karl Popper, *The Open Society and Its Enemies* (Princeton: Princeton University Press, 2013), 581.

According to Karl Popper, the paradox of tolerance means that "if we extend unlimited tolerance even to those who are intolerant, if we are not prepared to defend a tolerant society against the onslaught of the intolerant, then the tolerant will be destroyed, and tolerance with them... We should therefore claim, in the name of tolerance, the right not to tolerate the intolerant. We should claim that any movement preaching intolerance places itself outside the law, and we should consider incitement to intolerance and persecution as criminal."

125.   Elizabeth Fenton, *Religious Liberties: Anti-Catholicism and Liberal Democracy in Nineteenth-Century U.S. Literature and Culture* (Oxford: Oxford University Press, 2011), 4.

126.   Portions of this are reprinted with permission, from Sarah Beth Kaufman, "The Criminalization of Muslims in the US, 2016," *Qualitative Sociology* 42, no. 4 (2019): 521–542; and Sarah Beth Kaufman and Hanna Niner, "Muslim Victimization in the Contemporary US: Clarifying the Racialization Thesis," *Critical Criminology* 27, no. 3 (2019): 485–502.

127.   See the Pew Research report, Besheer Mohamed, "A New Estimate of the U.S. Muslim Population. Pew Research Center," January 6, 2016, https://www.pewresearch.org/fact-tank/2016/01/06/a-new-estimate-of-the-u-s-muslim-population/.

128.   Frantz Fanon, *Black Skin, White Masks* (New York, NY: Grove Press, 1952 [1967]).

129.   Jocelyne Cesari, *Why the West Fears Islam: An Exploration of Muslims in Liberal Democracies* (New York, NY: Palgrave Macmillan, 2013); José Casanova, "Immigration and the New Religious Pluralism: A European Union/United States Comparison," in *Democracy and the New Religious Pluralism,* ed. Thomas Banchoff (New York: Oxford, 2007), 59–84.

130.   See for examples: Louise Cainkar, *Homeland Insecurity: The Arab American and Muslim American Experience After 9/11* (New York: Russell Sage Foundation, 2009); Amaney Jamal and Nadine Naber, eds., *Race and Arab Americans Before and After 9/11: From Invisible Citizens to Visible Subjects* (Syracuse, NY: Syracuse University Press, 2008); Junaid Rana, *Terrifying Muslims: Race and Labor in the South Asian Diaspora* (Durham, NC: Duke University Press, 2011); and Saher Selod, *Forever Suspect: Racialized Surveillance of Muslims in the War on Terror* (New Brunswick, NJ: Rutgers University Press, 2018). On religious identity as part of intersectional racializing experiences more generally, see Grace Yukich and

Penny Edgell, eds. *Religion as Raced: Understanding American Religion in the Twenty-First Century* (New York: New York University Press, 2020).

131. Michael Omi and Howard Winant, *Racial Formation in the United States: From the 1960s to the 1990s*, Second Edition (New York City, NY: Routledge, 1994).

132. See Yuko Kawai, "Stereotyping Asian Americans: The Dialectic of the Model Minority and the Yellow Peril," *Howard Journal of Communication* 16, no. 2 (2005): 109–130.

133. Valerie Jenness, "Explaining Criminalization: From Demography and Status Politics to Globalization and Modernization," *Annual Review of Sociology* 30 (2004): 147–171.

134. Selod, *Forever Suspect.*

135. On right-wing organizations, see Christopher Bail, *Terrified: How Anti-Muslim Fringe Organizations Became Mainstream* (Princeton, NJ: Princeton University Press, 2015); and Michael Emerson and Christian Smith. *Divided by Faith: Evangelical Religion and the Problem of Race in America.* (New York: Oxford University Press, 2000).

136. George Morgan and Scott Poynting, eds. *Global Islamophobia: Muslims and Moral Panic in the West* (New York, NY: Routledge, 2012).

137. See in particular Chapter 3 of Bonilla-Silva, Eduardo, *Racism Without Racists: Color-Blind Racism and the Persistence of Racial Inequality in the United States,* 4th ed. (Lanham, MD: Rowman & Littlefield, 2014).

138. Aurelien Mondon and Aaron Winter, "Articulations of Islamophobia: From the Extreme to the Mainstream?" *Ethnic and Racial Studies* 40, no. 13 (2017): 2151–2179.

139. Jael Silliman and Annanya Bhattacharjee, *Policing the National Body: Sex, Race, and Criminalization.* (Cambridge, MA: South End Press, 2002).

140. Documented by Aditi Bhatia and Christopher Jenks, "Fabricating the American Dream in U.S. Media Portrayals of Syrian Refugees: A Discourse Analytical Study," *Discourse and Communication* 12, no. 3 (2016): 221–239.

141. Paul DiMaggio and Walter Powell, "The Iron Cage Revisited: Institutional Isomorphism and Collective Rationality in Organizational Fields," *American Sociological Review* 48, no. 2 (1983): 147–160.

142. For details, see Brian Levin, "Hate Crime Analysis and Forecast for 2016/2017," *Center for the Study of Hate Crime and Extremism* (2018), available at https://csbs.csusb.edu/sites/csusb_csbs/files/Final%20Hate%20Crime%2017%20Status%20Report%20pdf.pdf.

ACKNOWLEDGMENTS

All works of art and science are collaborations, and ours especially. The slim volume belies the many people that enabled it.

Major funding for the project was provided by the Andrew W. Mellon Foundation; Trinity University Office of the President (Danny Anderson); Trinity University Office of the Vice President (Deneese Jones); Humanities Texas; Dr. GP and Winkey Singh of the Sikh Spirit Foundation, San Antonio; and CAIR-San Antonio (Council of American-Islamic Relations).

We also thank: Stacey Connelly: Professor, Director, and dramaturg extraordinaire; Trinity University President Danny Anderson and Vice President Deneese Jones, unending supporters of this project in word and deed; four outstanding undergraduate researchers: Iris Baughman, Matt Long, Hanna Niner, and Van Wagner; William Razvi, Sam Gilliam, and the Arts @ Rec team for essential feedback on early versions of the script; and actor Josh Segovia, for his extraordinary commitment to "Chris," which inspired us in every performance.

We are grateful to family, colleagues, and friends who offered additional expertise and encouragement: Marsha Christ, Christine Drennon, Anne Hargrove, Ronnie and Phil Kaufman, Marsha Krassner, Sarwat Hussein, Rob Lerman and Kristin Metz, Tahir Naqvi, Mustafa Noor, Moina Noor, Judith Norman, Charley Price, and Sussan Siavoshi; our departmental homes in Sociology/Anthropology and Communication, especially with the leadership of Jennifer Henderson, David Spener, and Jennifer Mathews; our colleagues at Spelman College and Morehouse College Aku Kadogo, Mansa Bilal Mark King, Rebecca Kumar; direct Vincent Hardy; videographer/director Nathan Christ and Albert Salinas; Rebecca Snedecker, Director of the Center for Study of the Gulf South at Tulane University; KJ Sanchez at University of Texas Department of Theater and Dance; Todd Green at Luther College; Hannah Sullivan of the Bridge Initiative at Georgetown University; Mark Dennis and Hanan Hammad at Texas Christian University; Tiffany Puett, Executive Director of the Institute for Diversity and Civic Life; and the Trinity University Humanities Collective under the leadership of Ruben Dupertuis and Tim O'Sullivan.

We also gratefully acknowledge the many people who contributed to the first performances of *To Be Honest*, including the staff of the McNay Art Museum, led by Kate Carey; Texas Public Radio's San Antonio team and their "Dare to Listen" campaign; the organizers of San Antonio's "Dream Week;" staff and production teams at the Carver Cultural Center of San Antonio and the Tobin Center for the Performing Arts; Dhawn B. Martin and the SoL Center, University Presbyterian Church; WOAI's Taylor Mobley; Omar Rachid from the Victoria Islamic Center, TX; Tino Gallegos and the City of San Antonio Immigrant Welcome week; *The San Antonio Express-News*, and Trinity University community members Allie Butemeyer, James Bynum, Linda Campbell, Katie Carpenter, Debra Chick, Kory Cook, Irma DeLeon, Aaron Delwiche, Mary Margaret Herring, Lupita Puente, Peggy Sundermeyer, and Pat Ullmann.

Finally, we extend our thanks to the staff at Trinity University Press under the leadership of Tom Payton; and Kate Schubert, the very best editor a team could ever want.

A previous version of Chapter 5 was published in the journal *Qualitative Sociology* as: Kaufman, Sarah Beth. "The Criminalization of Muslims in the United States, 2016," 42, no. 4 (2020): 521–542. doi.org/10.1007 /s11133-019-09435-x, reprinted with permission.

CPSIA information can be obtained
at www.ICGtesting.com
Printed in the USA
JSHW042023110222
22866JS00001B/1

9 781595 349514